To the memory of Ferd, Greenie, and Jeff:

Ferdinand La France,
Greenleaf T. Chase,
Geoffrey Carleton.

Gone, but their stories live on.

Illustration by Jerry Russell

Adirondack Birding

60 Great Places to Find Birds

BY JOHN M.C. PETERSON
AND GARY N. LEE

WITH COLOR PHOTOGRAPHS
BY JEFF NADLER

LOST POND PRESS
Saranac Lake, N.Y.
2008

Published by **Lost Pond Press**
40 Margaret St., Saranac Lake, NY 12983
www.lostpondpress.com

Adirondack
Mountain Club

Distributed by **Adirondack Mountain Club**
814 Goggins Road
Lake George, NY 12845-4117
www.adk.org

Design by Susan Bibeau
Beehive Productions, Saranac Lake, NY

Maps by Matthew Paul

Illustrations by Jerry Russell and Mike Storey

Front-cover photos:
Black-backed Woodpecker by Jeff Nadler. www.jnphoto.net
Lake George by Carl Heilman II. www.carlheilman.com

Back-cover photos:
Bloomingdale Bog birder by Susan Bibeau
Bicknell's Thrush by Jeff Nadler

Jeff Nadler took most of the inside photos of birds, including all those in color. Carl Heilman II contributed a number of landscape photos.

ISBN: 978-0-9789254-3-7

Library of Congress Control Number: 2008936979

Printed in Canada by Transcontinental Press

Acknowledgments

The authors wish to express their gratitude to editor Phil Brown of Lost Pond Press for his encouragement and vision. He often went far beyond his editorial duty in checking facts on the ground, and any remaining errors of omission or commission are ours, not his. Space limitations prohibit thanking all of our birding companions who explored the sixty sites in this book with us over the years, but they know who they are. Friends who helped substantially in specific queries from the authors deserve mention, however, and include Dorothy Crumb, Charlcie Delahanty, Thomas Dudones, Judith Heintz, Gordon Howard, William Krueger, Theodore Mack, Brian McAllister, Melanie McCormack, Matthew Medler, William Purcell, Dana Rohleder, David Rutkowski, Thomas Salo, and Gerald Smith.

In addition, the editor wishes to acknowledge several people who answered his queries and offered suggestions: Larry Master, Joan Collins, Mona Bearor, and several folks at DEC, including Ken Kogut and Joe Racette. He thanks Dick Beamish, Tom Woodman, and Betsy Dirnberger of the *Adirondack Explorer* for their proofreading and encouragement.

The visual talents of many people enhanced the artistry of this book. The authors are grateful to Jeff Nadler for his superb bird photographs and to Carl Heilman II for his equally superb landscape shots. We also wish to thank others who contributed photos: the Adirondack Council, the Paul Smiths VIC, Nancy Ford, John Thaxton, John Mitchell, Mike Virtanen, Peter Post, and Kurt K. Burnham. Historical images came from the Harvard Library, Hobart and William Smith Colleges, and the Adirondack Room of the Saranac Lake Free Library. Thanks to Matthew Paul for his hand-drawn maps, Jerry Russell for his droll cartoons, and Mike Storey for his deft drawings. Susan Bibeau deserves much credit for pulling all the elements together in an attractive book design. She also contributed some fine photographs.

We also are grateful to the Adirondack Mountain Club for agreeing to distribute the book.

An undertaking of this scope was at times a trial—not to the authors, for whom the labor was a joy—but to their long-suffering spouses. For their patience and love, we offer heartfelt thanks to Karen Lee and Susan French Peterson.

Preface

Adirondack Birding is something new: a comprehensive guide to birding hot spots throughout the 5.8-million-acre Adirondack Park (and a few just outside it). The book strives to meet the needs of the modern birder, from the feeder-watcher eager to explore wild habitats to the veteran lister in search of boreal birds or rare transients. During research for the two New York State Breeding Bird Atlas projects (1980-85 and 2000-05), the authors visited almost all of the 690 "birding blocks," each comprising twenty-five square kilometers, in the Adirondack Mountains and Champlain Valley. For this book, we selected sixty sites that reflect the region's rich diversity of habitat and avifauna, from Lake Champlain (elevation 95 feet) to Mount Marcy (5,344 feet), from lowland bogs to the Tug Hill Plateau, from winding rivers to grassy fields.

You'll find birding suggestions for all seasons, whether you're keen on climbing a mountain to look for the reclusive Bicknell's Thrush in spring, paddling through a marsh to hear the unusual *pomp-er-lunk* of the American Bittern, observing a flock of Snow Geese feeding in a field during fall migration, or skiing through the woods listening to the songs of crossbills in the spruces. Our maps and directions will help you get there.

I should note here that although the book contains many remarkable color photographs of birds taken by Jeff Nadler, this is not a guide to identifying avifauna. Plenty of other books already serve that function.

All told, more than three hundred avian species have been documented in the Adirondack Park. No birder has yet seen three hundred species here, but several are closing in on that number. The sheer variety of the birdlife rivals that found anywhere in the Northeast, making up with boreal specialties what the region may lack in pelagic birds or rare transients and accidentals.

Our sixty sites target the species of most interest to birders who visit or live in the Adirondacks. Broadly, these are the boreal birds, rare migrants, and winter visitors, as well as such charismatic species as the Bald Eagle and Common Loon. If the southeastern section of the Park seems underrepresented, this is because much of its forestland is characterized by pine, hemlock, and hardwoods, with an avifauna easily found outside the Park.

As far as birders are concerned, the vast territory covered by this book can be divided in two: the Adirondack uplands and mountains and, to the east, the Champlain Valley. As a longtime resident of the Elizabethtown area, I have done most of my birding in the valley and the eastern Adirondacks. Gary Lee, a retired state forest ranger, does most of his in the central and western Adirondacks, where he resides. Between us, we've got the Park covered—as much as it's possible to cover 5.8 million acres.

The Adirondacks proper offer not only high summits with arctic vegetation and subalpine forests, but also lowland bogs and fens, marshy rivers and streams, and hundreds of lakes and ponds ringed by evergreens or boggy shores. Many boreal birds, rarely seen elsewhere in the state, are found in one or more of these habitats. They include Spruce Grouse, American Three-toed and Black-backed Woodpeckers, Olive-sided and Yellow-bellied Flycatchers, Philadelphia Vireo, Gray Jay, Boreal Chickadee, Ruby-crowned Kinglet, and Bicknell's Thrush. Northern warblers, which feed on spruce budworms, also breed in the Park (and show up outside it during migration), with the colorful males in full song in summer. These species include Tennessee, Cape May, Palm, Bay-breasted, Blackpoll, and Wilson's Warblers. Other sought-after northern birds include Lincoln's Sparrow, Rusty Blackbird, and White-winged Crossbill.

The Champlain Valley, separated from the mountains by a strip of foothills, has a milder climate and more southern flora. The valley provides a highway for migrants, a tunnel between the Adirondacks to the west and Green Mountains to the east. On the New York side, as hot air rises from dark, plowed fields, an updraft is created against the wall of hills and mountains to the west, offering lift to weary wings, especially for raptors (many birders hike to summits and ridges to observe hawk migrations). Not everyone will see an albatross wing northward past Crown Point (as happened May 8, 1994), but the list of rarities seen in the valley is impressive and gets longer each year. Black Scoter, Black-headed Gull, Black Tern, Black Skimmer, and Black Guillemot have all been spotted recently. Not all rarities are migrants, as Wilson's Phalarope and Nelson's Sharp-tailed Sparrow have been recorded as breeding at the Chazy Riverlands.

Both transients and breeding birds tend to gather in swamps and marshes, especially at estuaries and deltas where streams and rivers enter Lake Champlain or inland waterbodies. Champlain's deep bays offer refuge for waterfowl. Its large peninsulas serve as migrant traps, concentrating passerines in spring and fall. One of them, Crown Point, hosted twenty-three different warblers alone in May 2007. Offshore islands, most notably the Four Brothers and Valcour Island, provide security for geese, ducks, mergansers, cormorants, herons, egrets, night-herons, and ibises. Beaches and mudflats host numerous species of transient shorebirds from July until late fall. The valley's hayfields and pastures also turn up many interesting birds, among them Northern Harrier, Short-eared Owl, Horned Lark, Sedge Wren, Vesper and Savannah Sparrows, Bobolink, and Eastern Meadowlark, with American Pipit, Lapland Longspur, and Snow Bunting found in migration and during winter.

As birders, we have a special responsibility to protect birds and their habitat. Respect the sites described in this guidebook. Readers are encouraged to use it as a starting point and to discover other hidden wonders of the Adirondack-Champlain region on their own. The birds are there; they need only to be found.

John M.C. Peterson

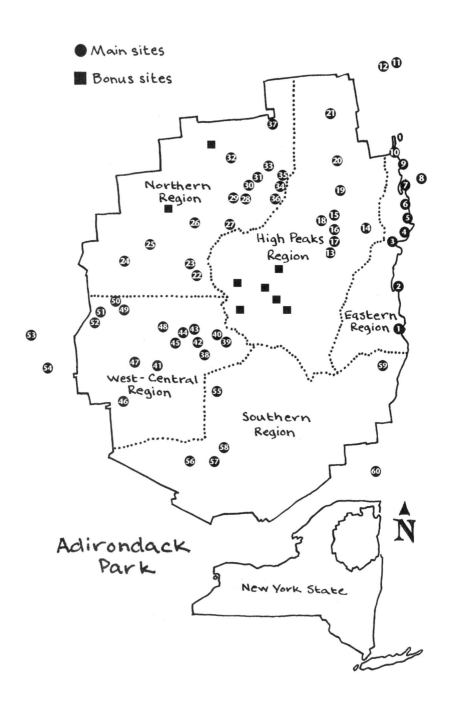

Main sites

Bonus sites

Northern Region

High Peaks Region

Eastern Region

West-Central Region

Southern Region

Adirondack Park

New York State

N

Contents

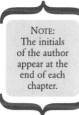

NOTE:
The initials
of the author
appear at the
end of each
chapter.

List of Color Photographs

Although *Adirondack Birding* is not an identification guidebook, it does contain color photographs of forty-six species taken by Jeff Nadler. They include many of the boreal birds and other species of special interest to enthusiasts. The species represent a variety of habitats.

The following photos appear after Page 56

PLATE 1: Boreal Chickadee.

PLATE 2: American Bittern, Virginia Rail, Wood Duck, Ring-necked Duck.

PLATE 3: Northern Harrier, Northern Parula, Savannah Sparrow, Bobolink.

PLATE 4: Bonaparte's Gull, Pectoral Sandpiper.

PLATE 5: Blue-headed Vireo, Philadelphia Vireo, Red-eyed Vireo.

PLATE 6: Bohemian Waxwing, Rough-legged Hawk, Snow Bunting, Short-eared Owl.

PLATE 7: Blackpoll Warbler, Mourning Warbler, Blackburnian Warbler, Pine Warbler.

PLATE 8: Scarlet Tanager, Barred Owl, Hermit Thrush, Ovenbird.

The following photos appear after Page 168

PLATE 9: Common Loon.

PLATE 10: Spruce Grouse, Olive-sided Flycatcher, Yellow-bellied Flycatcher.

PLATE 11: Osprey, Merlin, Bald Eagle.

PLATE 12: Gray Jay.

PLATE 13: Bicknell's Thrush.

PLATE 14: Tennessee Warbler, Bay-breasted Warbler, Cape May Warbler, Yellow Palm Warbler.

PLATE 15: Rusty Blackbird, White-throated Sparrow, Lincoln's Sparrow, Ruby-crowned Kinglet.

PLATE 16: Evening Grosbeak, American Three-toed Woodpecker, White-winged Crossbill.

Using this Book

BIRDING ETIQUETTE. Respect the birds and their environment. Keep back from nests, nesting colonies, roosts, and display areas. The American Birding Association urges restraint in the use of recordings to attract birds. Because they can distress birds, recordings should not be used to attract species that are classified as endangered, threatened, or of special concern or that are locally rare. Nor should they be used at heavily birded locations. Photographers should use artificial light sparingly. As much as possible, stay on trails and roads to avoid disturbing habitat.

GEOGRAPHIC REGIONS. The sixty birding sites are grouped into five geographical regions. For the most part, these correspond to regions delineated by the Adirondack Mountain Club (ADK) for its series of Adirondack Trails guidebooks. Three sites inside the Adirondack Park–Lyon, Pillsbury, and Tongue mountains–are exceptions to the rule. The book also describes five sites that lie just outside the Park. These were placed within the most suitable ADK region. Cross references to sites are boldfaced.

GETTING THERE. The book contains page maps and directions for every site. For planning trips and driving around the Park, birders may want to consult National Geographic's color topographical maps of the Adirondack Park, part of the Trails Illustrated series. A set of five covers the whole Park. They show roads, hiking trails, lean-tos, and canoe put-ins. The trail numbers correspond to trail numbers in ADK guidebooks. The maps also differentiate between private and state land. The maps can be ordered online from National Geographic or the Adirondack Mountain Club.

ADIRONDACK PARK. It's often said that the 5.8 million-acre Adirondack Park is the largest park in the Lower 48 states. However, only about half the land belongs to the forever-wild Forest Preserve. The rest is privately owned. The state has purchased conservation easements on many tracts of commercial timberland that permit some public recreation, but most of the Park's private land is not open. If you venture onto easement lands, be sure you know the rules. Not all easement lands are open to the public. Except at state campgrounds, there is no charge for using the Forest Preserve and easement lands.

WILDERNESS PREPAREDNESS. Anytime you go into the wilderness, be prepared to spend the night in case you get lost or injured. Carry a map and compass, water bottle and filter, extra food, first-aid kit, knife, headlamp or flashlight, extra clothing (including rain gear), space blanket or emergency shelter, whistle, and matches or a lighter. Leave the forest as you found it. Carry out trash–yours and that left behind by others.

DEC. The state Department of Environmental Conservation is responsible for managing the Forest Preserve, including the maintenance of trails (which are marked by plastic disks). In an emergency, call the department's twenty-four-hour hotline at 518-891-0235, but don't count on cell phones to work in the wild. See the agency's Web site for more information about the Park. The department is referred to in most cases in this book as DEC.

* * *

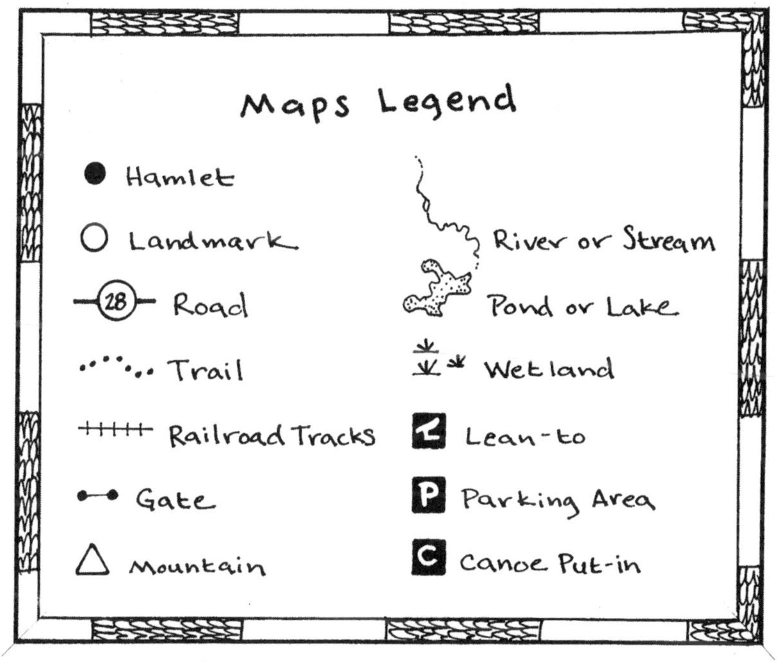

Maps Legend

- ● Hamlet
- ○ Landmark
- —(28)— Road
- ·······.. Trail
- +++++ Railroad Tracks
- •—• Gate
- △ Mountain

- River or Stream
- Pond or Lake
- ⅄⅄ Wetland
- ◪ Lean-to
- 🅿 Parking Area
- 🅲 Canoe Put-in

The page maps use the symbols shown above. In some cases, two or three birding sites are shown on a single map. If a site chapter lacks a map, the reader will be referred to the appropriate map in the driving directions for that site. Usually, trailheads and put-ins are indicated by a "P" in a black box. Occasionally, a "C" is used to show a canoe route or put-in. All of the maps were drawn by hand by Matthew Paul of Saranac Lake.

A History of Adirondack Birding

By John M.C. Peterson

Birding has exploded in recent years. In the United States alone, there are now more than forty-six million birders, who spend many billions of dollars a year in a quest to add to their life lists. Once, the goal of seeing seven hundred species in North America (excluding Latin America) seemed unattainable, until that barrier was broken by Joseph Taylor, a wealthy birder from Rochester and Lake Placid, in the 1970s. By 2006, the list of North American birders who had found eight hundred species was thirty strong, followed by another 279 who had broken the old seven-hundred mark.

Most of the early explorers and naturalists of the Adirondack-Champlain region never would have imagined that birding would become a leisure pastime. They were driven by a scientific curiosity to learn what was here and to provide an ornithological record for future generations, based upon narratives, specimens, egg sets and nests, and annotated species lists. To them we owe a considerable debt, especially since it was not until the second half of the last century that a full picture of the region's birds began to develop.

The first notable regional work, translated and published in Great Britain in 1770-71, described the travels of a Swedish botanist into New France in 1749, prior to the French and Indian War. The book was *Travels into North America*, the translator was English naturalist John Reinhold Forster (he of Forster's Tern), and the Swede was Pehr Kalm (1716-79), baptized Petter, and often called "Peter" in English. Kalm is sometimes described as a disciple of Carolus Linnaeus, founder of the Linnaean system of scientific nomenclature, but while at the University of Uppsala he was also a student of Anders Celsius (of thermometer fame). Sent to North America to collect plants of economic significance to Sweden, he became friends with John Bartram and Benjamin Franklin, enjoying a last supper of yams with Franklin in Philadelphia before setting out for New York, Albany, and Montreal.

On June 29, 1749, his party was nearing South Bay of Lake Champlain and the Drowned Lands just to the north. "We saw immense numbers of those wild pigeons flying in the woods. . . . They have their nests in the trees here," Kalm writes, "and almost all the night make a great noise and cooing in the trees, where they roost. The *Frenchmen* shot a great number of them." The Passenger Pigeon is long gone, but it has been memorialized in the Adirondacks by such toponyms as Pigeon Hill, Pigeon Roost, and Pigeon Lake.

Passenger Pigeon

Arriving in New France at Fort St. Frederic at the tip of Crown Point on July 2, Kalm found that the officers were already making "collections of curiosities in the animal kingdom." He arrived at the height of French scientific interest, commenting, "I found that the people of distinction, in general here, had a much greater taste for natural history and other parts of literature than the *English* colonies, where it was every body's sole care and employment to scrape a future together, and where the sciences were held in universal contempt."

Setting out for Montreal on July 19, he observed, "Fourteen *French* miles from fort *St. Frederic* we saw four large islands in the lake, which is here about six *French* miles broad." He is referring to the Four Brothers on Lake Champlain, but he makes no mention of any waterbirds on or around the islands. Kalm was the first trained naturalist to describe the region but confined most of his observations to flora and geology, although he later authored two papers (in Swedish only) on the Passenger Pigeon.

Almost a century would pass, with New France and British America fading in memory, before a major work on this state's birds would be published. The year 1844 saw the appearance of *Zoology of New-York, or, the New-York Fauna, Part II: Birds*, by Portuguese-born James Ellsworth De Kay (1792-1852), a graduate of the University of Edinburgh and editor of the first paper presented by John James Audubon. Published by the State Museum, the tome is based upon the five-year New York Natural History Survey of 1836-40, a forebear of today's statewide breeding-bird atlases. The 353 quarto pages include descriptions of 309 species found in the state. Information on birds of the Great North Woods was limited in the early nineteenth century and still based in part on the testimony of residents, so while many of the accounts of Adirondack birds are accurate (Common Loon breeding on Raquette Lake, for example), other entries are incorrect. De Kay wrote that Tundra Swan formerly bred in Hamilton and Herkimer counties, stating, "The outlet of Lake Paskungamet, or Tupper's Lake, was specified as a spot to which they were particularly attached." Even if this swan was more common in early days, there is no evidence of its nesting

Theodore Roosevelt

here. Nevertheless, his effort marked the beginning of an era of serious state and regional bird study, and De Kay remained the standard for the rest of the nineteenth century.

Three decades later, in August 1874, fifteen-year-old Theodore Roosevelt Jr. (1858-1919) began a list of birds seen and collected ("Pine Siskin. One specimen got, August 27th, 1874") while vacationing with his family near the Saint Regis Lakes. He continued collecting birds the following August ("Barred Owl. One shot in August, 1875. Probably not very rare"). Teddy entered Harvard in 1876 and missed a season in the Adirondacks, but in 1877, at eighteen, he returned for a third time from June 22 to July 9, joined during the last week of June by seventeen-year old Henry Davis Minot (1859-90) of Boston, who shared his enthusiasm for birds. Later that year, they published a four-page pamphlet in New York City, *The Summer Birds of the Adirondacks in Franklin County, N.Y.*, an annotated list of ninety-seven species they had observed. Their summer-only studies had taken place mainly around the hamlet of Paul Smiths, Bay and Follensby Junior ponds, and Spitfire and Upper Saint Regis lakes, although they found a few open-country species near Malone. The Roosevelt-Minot list, the first compilation of Adirondack birds, has been reprinted several times, first in the *Roosevelt Wild Life Bulletin* (1923) and most recently in *Birds of Franklin County, New York* and on its accompanying *Birding Trail Map* (2006). This seminal work by two teenagers marks the beginning of listing here, both as a leisure activity and as an amateur contribution to science.

What was needed was a more complete list of birds, covering those found throughout the year and over the entire region. That task fell to Clinton Hart Merriam (1855-1942), son of a New York importer and banker. His father retired from business in 1864 and built a mansion west of the Adirondacks in Locust Grove, Lewis County, where Merriam spent his formative years. At fifteen, he went west with the Hayden Survey of 1871 that resulted in the creation of the first national park at Yellowstone, and he began writing about birds. In the same year, his father began serving the first of two terms (1871-75) as a Republican member of the U.S. House of Representatives from New York. Merriam began scientific studies at Yale, then moved to New York to pursue medicine at Columbia, becoming a founder and the first president of the Linnaean Society. On June 4, 1878, he and noted oologist C.L. Bagg found the first nest of American Three-toed Woodpecker in the state, near McKeever in Herkimer County, and collected the set of eggs. The following year, at twenty-three, he moved back to Locust Grove, where he practiced medicine until 1885 and continued his scientific writing. From 1878-79 he published a three-part article on the birds of Lewis County, giving details of fifteen species. The rest of his twenties were spent in Locust Grove working on two major projects.

The first was his "Preliminary List of Birds Ascertained to Occur in the Adirondack Region, Northeastern New York" and two addenda. These appeared in the *Bulletin of the Nuttall Ornithological Club* in 1881 and 1882. A third addendum was published in the first issue of the successor journal, *The Auk*, in 1884. His final list included 211 species, the last entry a Black Tern collected at Schroon Lake. In the original list, Merriam's discussion of Nashville Warbler concludes, "Also given by Roosevelt and Minot from Franklin Co.," his only mention of their work among the 211 entries. His geographic scope extended from Lake George and Lake Champlain up to at least Plattsburgh in the east and as far as Lowville and Bangor to the west.

Merriam's second project was his monumental *The Mammals of the Adirondack Region, Northeastern New York*, published in two volumes from 1882-84. At thirty-one, Merriam left his medical practice to become the first head of the U.S. Department of Agriculture's Division of Economic Ornithology and Mammalogy, predecessor of

John William Hill's illustration of an Ovenbird appeared in Zoology of New-York (1844).

Saranac Lake Free Library

the U.S. Fish and Wildlife Service, a position he held from 1886 until 1910. He also served as president of the American Ornithologists' Union from 1900-03. Theodore Roosevelt (by then the nation's president) became a great supporter of Merriam. In 1910, after TR left office, Merriam served as a research associate at the Smithsonian Institution for nearly three decades (1910-39). He died in Berkeley, Calif., in March 1942. Merriam deserves to be remembered for compiling the first annotated list of all birds known in the Adirondack-Champlain region.

The first detailed description of a birding area (and thus a forerunner to this book) appeared in the journal *Ornithologist and Oologist* in 1888: "A Visit to the Four Brothers, Lake Champlain," by Alvah H.B. Jordan (1865-1942) of Willsboro, son of a Boston dry-goods merchant. After attending public schools in Boston, Jordan went on to a career in the paper industry. When twenty-one, he set sail for the islands, "accompanied by my ornithological partner," on May 22, 1887. They found the woods alive with warblers and the air discordant with the screams of the Herring Gull, and he listed twenty-nine species found by the following day. His partner was twenty-year-old Augustus Gibson Paine Jr. (1866-1947), son of a wealthy paper manufacturer. When Champlain Fiber & Pulp went belly up in 1885, Augustus Sr. wound up owning the company and summoned young Gus home from studies in England to run the plant. Gus, who had an interest in birds, was the co-author (with Lewis B. Woodruff) of "Birds of Central Park, New York: A Preliminary List," published in *Forest and Stream* in 1886. He soon teamed up with Jordan on birding expeditions. For many years the cabinets of study specimens and egg sets they collected were housed in the Paine Memorial Library in Willsboro, along with the large ledger, field notebook, collecting gun, and antique decoys. The study skins–which included a Passenger Pigeon collected by Paine at Willsboro October 9, 1891–are now deposited at the American Museum of Natural History in New York. Jordan later became an officer of Everett Pulp & Paper on Puget Sound, and Paine went on to run a paper empire from Manhattan. Jordan's article was reprinted at Elizabethtown in 1987. That same year, a party of six birders paid tribute to Paine and Jordan by making a centennial visit to

Loons painted by Louis Agassiz Fuertes for Birds of New York *(1910-14)*

Elon Howard Eaton

the Four Brothers May 22-23. This latter-day crew identified thirty-nine species, setting a challenge for birders in May of 2087.

A thorough account of a seven-week birding expedition in the Adirondacks a century ago can be found in *Birds of New York*, by Elon Howard Eaton (1866-1935). The State Museum published this magnum opus, a two-volume successor to De Kay, from 1910-1914. The county lists, 411 species accounts, and range maps remain invaluable and are still cited today. Also, the plates by Louis Agassiz Fuertes are greatly admired (and sadly collected from broken volumes). The introduction includes Eaton's essay on "The Mount Marcy Region," describing a survey that the author made with "his assistants" from June 15 until the first week of August 1905. (Joseph Taylor, a noted birder, said the assistants were Eaton's teenage students from Canandaigua Academy and included Taylor's father, Tom Taylor of Rochester.) If you are familiar with any of the following place names, this nine-page account is most rewarding: Ausable Swamp, Bartlett Ridge, Beede Pond, Clear Pond, Boreas Ponds, Mount Colvin, Elizabethtown, Elk Lake, Flowed Lands, Mount Haystack, John Brown's Grave, Keene Valley, Mount Marcy, Middle Saranac Lake, Polliwog Pond, Mount Skylight, Spruce Hill, Upper Ausable, and Whiteface Mountain. Eaton received his undergraduate and master's degrees from the University of Rochester (which later granted him an honorary doctorate). He taught in secondary schools for fifteen years, then served as professor of biology at Hobart and William Smith Colleges in Geneva from 1908-35, as well as holding the posts of state ornithologist and curator of the State Museum. His son, Stephen W. Eaton, a Hobart graduate, authored many of the species accounts in *The Atlas of Breeding Birds in New York State* (1988).

A detailed description of Adirondack birding in the early years of the twentieth century was provided by noted ornithologist Aretas Andrews Saunders, who died in 1970. Widely traveled, he was a prolific writer, his contributions to *The Auk* spanning a half-century, from about 1908-58. His *Bird Song*, published by the State Museum in 1929, reflected one of his passions; he later made use of technology to help develop the sonogram. Saunders spent two summers in the Adirondacks. From July 2 to August 17, 1925, he stayed most nights at the Wood Farm on Heart Lake Road (now known as Adirondak Loj Road), exploring the MacIntyre Range and Mount Marcy, except for a day spent in Franklin County. The following year he stayed at the Lake Clear Inn from July 9 to August 13, exploring the St. Regis Lakes region as far south as Saranac Inn. The report of his trips, with comments on 121 species of summer birds, appeared in the *Roosevelt Wild Life Bulletin* in 1929, which included two topographic maps of his study sites, as well as the second reprint of the Roosevelt-Minot list. Saunders explained, "I have included in my total list, not only the species I personally have found in these regions, but also those that were found by Roosevelt and Minot, and some that are reported by Eaton from the vicinity of Mt. Marcy." With a birder's eye, Saunders took sixty-eight photographs to illustrate his 185-page work, allowing us a glimpse back in time to see places like the Heart Lake Road as it looked almost a quarter-century after the fire of 1903.

Just as Saunders was preparing to set off for the Lake Clear Inn, sixteen-year-old Geoffrey Carleton (1909-98) of New York City was making a note of a late transient Blackpoll Warbler near the family camp, Juniper, on Cobble Hill in Elizabethtown on June 4, 1926. Carleton, who went to Princeton, published his first article in *The Auk*, "Notes from Essex County, N.Y.," in 1935. A librarian, he received bachelor's and master's degrees from Columbia in 1941 and then served in the Army in World War II. He was employed by City College of New York, Brooklyn Public Library, and New York University Library. While living in the city, Carleton served—as Clinton Hart Merriam had—as president of the Linnaean Society, and he wrote *The Birds of Central and Prospect Parks* (1947, revised 1958).

Retiring to Juniper in the 1960s, Carleton continued to maintain and add to his records of Essex County birds. In 1976, he published *Birds of Essex County, New York*. This first edition provided details on status, arrival and departure dates, and maxima (most sighted in one place)—verified by place

Neal Smith and Geoffrey Carleton, 1958

and observer—for 255 species. A second edition in 1980 listed 270 species, and a posthumous third edition in 1999 described 310 species, including the 272nd bird personally sighted by Carleton in Essex County, a dark-phased Swainson's Hawk migrating north at Witherbee on June 10, 1997. His monumental effort inspired similar books on the birds of Clinton County (Warren 1979 and Mitchell & Krueger 1997), Hamilton County (John M.C. Peterson and Gary Lee, 2004), and Franklin County (Peterson, 2006). Everyone from Gus Paine to Roger Peterson knew Jeff Carleton, and Carleton himself could remember Ludlow Griscom, the dean of American birdwatchers, his dark suitcoat buttoned, leading his disciples from the American Museum of Natural History into Central Park. Carleton saw—and indeed helped foster—the transition of birding from a purely scientific pursuit to a leisure activity, from professional ornithology into a new era of citizen science.

During the twentieth century, Carleton and others noticed the northward movement of a number of more southern species into the region. Northern Cardinal appeared at Wadhams in 1933, followed after World War II by the first regional Carolina Wren in 1952 and Prairie Warbler in 1955. The list grew: Northern Mockingbird, 1960; Cattle Egret, '62; Golden-winged Warbler, '64; Willow Flycatcher, '70; Tufted Titmouse, '73; Blue-gray Gnatcatcher and House Finch, '74; Worm-eating Warbler, '79; Blue-winged Warbler,'81; Cerulean Warbler, '83; Snowy Egret and Red-bellied Woodpecker, '84; Glossy Ibis, '90, and Fish Crow, '94. All of these arrived via the Champlain corridor, but many have now penetrated more boreal portions of the Adirondacks. Carleton's suspicion that moderating temperatures were at the root of these northward range expansions has become conventional wisdom in the twenty-first century.

Recreational birders can do a great service to our understanding of changes to the natural world by reporting all significant sightings to the regional editor of *The Kingbird*, the state journal of record published by the New York State Ornithological Association. The oddity of today may well be tomorrow's backyard breeder. Tracking the locations and numbers of boreal birds is no less important, as forest types change in response to global and regional temperature changes. Bear in mind the famous photo of Earth taken from lunar orbit by the Apollo 8 astronauts in 1968. That blue orb is our only home. Birds can help us understand the changes taking place in our world. We can pay tribute to the great observers of the previous centuries by carrying on their work. ❋

Wilson's Snipe

Eastern Region

Champlain Valley's Avian Abundance

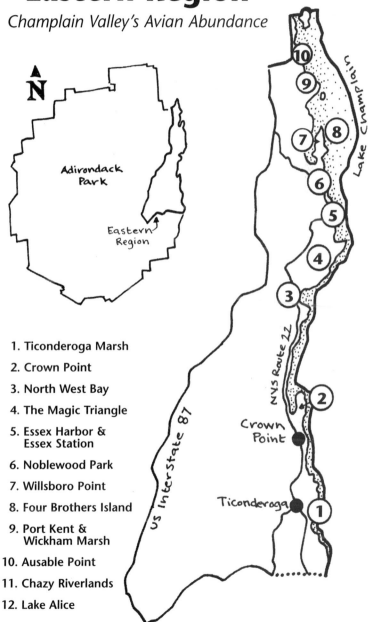

1. Ticonderoga Marsh
2. Crown Point
3. North West Bay
4. The Magic Triangle
5. Essex Harbor & Essex Station
6. Noblewood Park
7. Willsboro Point
8. Four Brothers Island
9. Port Kent & Wickham Marsh
10. Ausable Point
11. Chazy Riverlands
12. Lake Alice

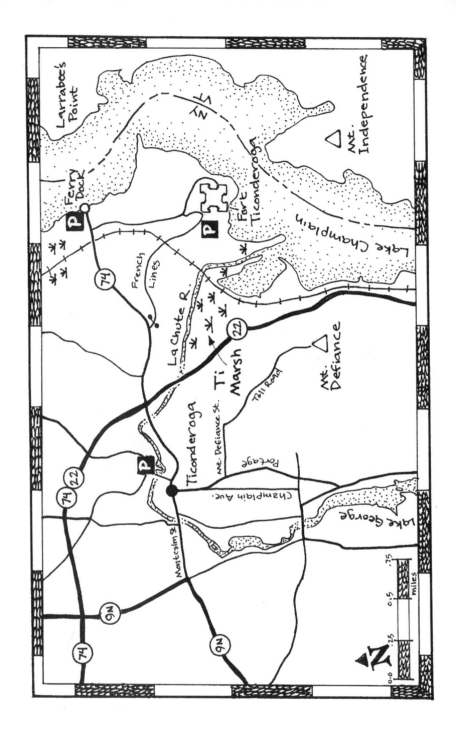

Ticonderoga Marsh

Explore the mouth of La Chute River, searching for Common Moorhen, Green Heron, Least Bittern, Wilson's Snipe, and other marsh birds. On the paddle downriver, listen for Yellow-throated Vireos and Red-bellied Woodpeckers in a bottomland forest.

DIRECTIONS: The marsh is reached by canoe or kayak. To launch in La Chute River, from the Liberty Monument traffic circle on NY 9N in Ticonderoga, drive east on Montcalm Street for 0.7 miles, passing through downtown. Turn left on Tower Avenue and go about 250 yards to the end, crossing the river. Turn right on Burgoyne Road, then make a quick right into a park. Launch in the pool below the falls. A second launch site is located on Lake Champlain at the state boat launch near the Ticonderoga ferry landing. From the outskirts of the hamlet, take NY 74 east, passing Fort Ticonderoga and the Amtrak station en route to the landing.

The paddle to Ti Marsh, as locals call it, is about one and a half miles from either of the usual put-ins, and each trip is interesting in its own right. The La Chute River launch is just downstream from an attractive waterfall that once was hidden in the bowels of the old brick International Paper mill. Today the clear water flows unimpeded from the outlet of Lake George to Lake Champlain, a distance of about three miles. The flatwater trip from the launch to Champlain takes the paddler through quiet stretches of bottomland forest, interrupted only by startled Green Herons or the songs of Yellow-throated and Warbling Vireos. Listen, too, for Red-bellied Woodpecker. Five Common Moorhens lingered along the lower stretch

Bottomland forest on La Chute River

until late January 2007, dabbling and diving, but in nesting season most are found out in the marsh itself. Geoffrey Carleton first found moorhens breeding at Ti Marsh in the 1930s, and they have been seen regularly in the years since.

La Chute enters Ti Marsh just above the Canadian Pacific railway trestle. Entering channels through the sea of cattails, listen for the rattle of male Marsh Wrens and watch for their nests, most of them dummies. Follow the lakeshore east and north, and in May stop at the hawthorn grove just past the train tunnel, below a pasture and the Fort Ticonderoga parking lot. The low trees often harbor warblers. Blue-gray Gnatcatcher frequents this area, and Orchard Oriole was regular in the mid-1970s. Watch the shoreline below the fort walls for Wilson's Snipe and hope for the *coo-coo-coo* calls of Least Bittern in nearby cattails, first documented in the 1930s but last reported in May 1980. As many as six Black Terns could be found over the marsh into the 1970s, but the last sighting was in 1982. If time allows, paddle across to the south side of the marsh near the old Ticonderoga station and be alert for Gadwall among the other puddle ducks. Keep an eye on the sky for Osprey, Bald Eagle, and Northern Harrier, and in spring or fall watch for migrant hawks above 853-foot Mount Defiance near the fort. Over a hundred avian species nest near the village and marsh.

Photo by John Mitchell

Osprey

The paddle south from the ferry landing to Ti Marsh is about the same distance, but the main lake may be choppy or rough at times. Just to the north of the landing is another lakeshore marsh well worth exploring; this area opens early during ice-out and is always a good spot to check from the parking lot for migrant waterfowl. If the gate to Fort Ticonderoga is open, the entrance road into the fort offers excellent birding, with Pine Warbler in the conifers and Scarlet Tanager in hardwoods near the old French Lines of July 1758. —**JP**

② **Crown Point**

Stroll among ruins of two stone forts on the tip of a peninsula located in the middle of the Lake Champlain flyway. Over the years, birders have banded ninety-nine species at Crown Point, including twenty-six warblers, and seen such rarities as Yellow-nosed Albatross and Tufted Duck.

DIRECTIONS: From NY 9N (it's also NY 22 here) between Crown Point hamlet and Port Henry, turn east onto NY 903, following signs to the Crown Point Bridge to Vermont. Head east and then north for 4 miles and look for the Crown Point State Historic Site sign and entrance on the left, across from the restored ruins of the Light Infantry Redoubt and before a DEC campground.

This 360-acre state historic site at the tip of Crown Point peninsula is a New York State Bird Conservation Area and an Audubon Important Bird Area. If the entrance gate is closed, park across the highway and walk along the access road. If the gate is open, a modest entrance fee may be charged. Stop at the interpretive panels to read about birds and bird banding; they are located near the rest rooms, opposite the picnic pavilion. One panel includes a map that shows the birding trails and the location of the banding station. Continue to the parking lot between the ruins of Fort St. Frederic (French) and His Majesty's Fort at Crown Point (British). Visiting naturalist Pehr (Peter) Kalm found immense numbers of Passenger Pigeons nesting at the south end of the lake on his way to Fort St. Frederic in 1749,

Photo by Carl Heilman II

Ruins of the British fort at Crown Point

and pigeon bones were found in kitchen middens behind the Soldiers' Barracks. If the nearby museum is open, ask for "Birds of Crown Point State Historic Site," a checklist of species.

In winter, mixed waterfowl gather at open leads in the ice under the bridge, visible from the French fort. Rarities found at the tip of the peninsula have included Tufted Duck (Winter 2002-03), Yellow-nosed Albatross (May '94), Tricolored Heron (August '83), Glossy Ibis (May '99), Laughing Gull (August '93), Little Gull (October '86, May '96), Sabine's Gull (October '88), and Forster's Tern (April '94). From the British fort, walk uphill to the west through an old farmyard and into a grassy field. Straight ahead (west) through an old quarry is the eighteenth-century carriage road down to Bulwagga Bay; listen for Prairie Warbler or Clay-colored Sparrow in the cedar-juniper area near the quarry. From the bay, this trail swings left and back up to the banding station. Most birders don't go directly to the bay. They opt instead to turn left past the barns and follow a wide mown path directly to the banding station. The nearby low hawthorn thickets are long famous for warbler waves. The path continues to the south, passing cellar holes of the eighteenth-century village, a nineteenth-century limekiln, and Gage's Redoubt, at the top of the rise just beyond. Listen for a Black-billed Cuckoo, Red-bellied Woodpecker, Blue-gray Gnatcatcher, or Orchard Oriole. Continue south to a T-intersection with a dirt road at an open area known as Bobolink Field, good for grassland birds. A short right here leads down to Fossil Rock on Bulwagga Bay. Scan the bay for waterfowl and cormorants, enjoy the fossils, and check the Osprey platform to the right before returning.

As a northward-pointing peninsula, Crown Point is a natural migrant trap in spring, and the banding station, operated by the Crown Point Banding Association, has opened each May since 1976. Through 2008, a total of ninety-nine species and almost fifteen thousand birds have been banded. These include twenty-six species of warbler, plus "Brewster's" hybrid (1999), the "Yellow" Palm subspecies ('98), and even a bilateral gynandromorph Common Yellowthroat ('99), while Yellow-throated Warbler ('95) and Connecticut Warbler (May and August '96) have been seen only. Even Boreal Chickadee ('83) has turned up in the nets. Before leaving Crown Point, be sure to stop at the state campground across the highway to view the small bronze bust of *La Belle France* by Auguste Rodin set into the north side of the Champlain Monument, built above the site of the Grenadiers' Redoubt that once guarded these historic Champlain narrows. —JP

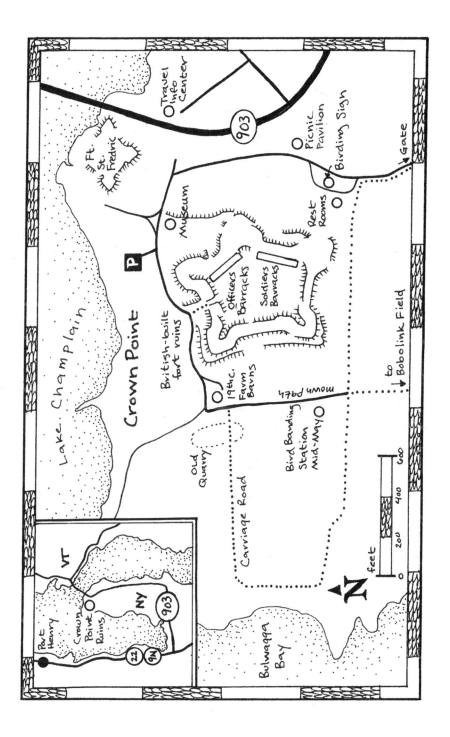

Travel Info Center

903

Picnic Pavilion

Birding Sign

Gate

Ft. St. Fredric

Museum

Rest Rooms

British-built fort ruins

P

Officers Barracks

Soldiers Barracks

Lake Champlain

Crown Point

19thc. Farm Barns

Old Quarry

mown path

to Bobolink Field

Bird Banding Station Mid-May

Carriage Road

N
feet
0   200   400   600

VT

Crown Point Ruins

NY

903

Port Henry

22   9N

Bulwagga Bay

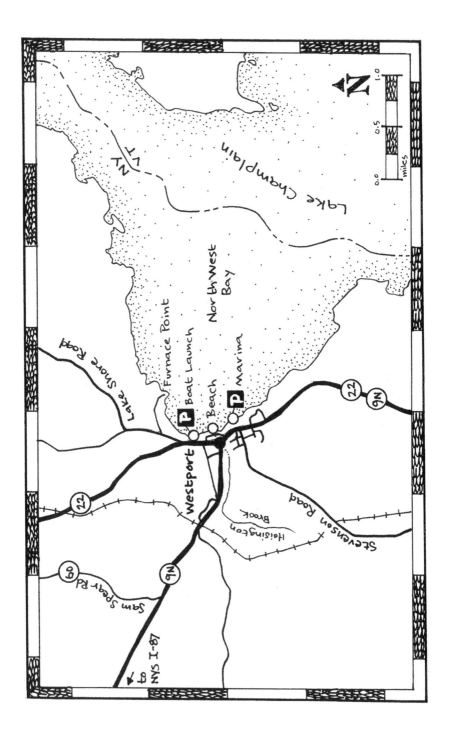

③ North West Bay

Scan one of the largest bays on Lake Champlain for a variety of ducks, scoters, loons, grebes, and many other birds. A number of rarities, such as Greater White-fronted Goose and Parasitic Jaeger, have been spotted here.

DIRECTIONS: At the north end of the hamlet of Westport on NY 22, start at the spacious parking lot of the Westport Boat Launch, marked by a DEC sign. Drive or walk south on 22 and take the second lane to the left leading to the sewer plant and beach. Then continue south on 22 over the highway bridge, taking an immediate left and steep downhill to the marina.

Westport is one of the most productive birding spots on Lake Champlain, well worth a visit whenever North West Bay is not frozen. Make stops at the state boat launch, sewer plant, beach, and marina, since each provides a different view of the shoreline and bay. Not every visit will produce a rarity, but the rather remarkable list of those found previously includes Greater White-fronted Goose (November 1996), Cackling Goose (January 2007), Eared Grebe (December 1976), Snowy Egret (May 1984), Tricolored Heron (May 1989), Piping Plover (August 1991), Willet (August 1975), Stilt Sandpiper (August 1987), Parasitic Jaeger (January 1999), Franklin's Gull (July 1984), Black Skimmer (June-July 2004), Black Guillemot (January 1978), Nelson's Sharp-tailed Sparrow (October 1983), and Yellow-headed Blackbird (March 1998). As these sightings suggest, an exciting discovery might be made in almost any month.

From the boat launch, scan the bay and main lake beyond with binoculars and spotting scope. During late winter the bay may be covered only with ice shanties, and in midsummer the only birds of note may be the flock of Mallards around the boat ramp and Ring-billed Gulls out on the bay. In late fall and early winter, however, North West Bay can be covered with mixed rafts of hundreds–often thousands–of waterfowl. Check the inshore puddle ducks for Gadwall, American Wigeon, or Northern Shoveler. Among the diving ducks, any of the three scoters (Black, Surf, or White-winged) is possible, and scan the rafts of Common Goldeneye carefully for a Barrow's Goldeneye. Common Loons and Horned Grebes tend to swim and dive farther out; use a scope to search for Red-throated Loon or Red-necked Grebe in their vicinity. Watch for Bald Eagles in winter.

Park just above the sewer plant and walk down to the shoreline to check the little bay to the north, then return and cross a small footbridge over Hoisington Brook to the public beach. Again walk down to the shoreline and check the mouth of the brook and marina area to the south. The willows

Photo by Phil Brown

A gathering of gulls at North West Bay

and brush along the length of Hoisington Brook, long favored by Yellow Warblers and where the Sharp-tailed Sparrow was found in 1983, continue to be cut back, leaving only stumps and stubs that then attempt to sucker into regrowth. Loads of sand have been added to the public beach. The effect has been to cover the shoreline mudflats with sand, and an area that had been a magnet for southbound shorebirds is sometimes bereft of birds today. But Solitary, Ruddy Turnstone, Least, Baird's, and Pectoral sand-pipers turned up in late August 2007, and all three phalaropes (Wilson's, Red-necked, Red) were found here into the 1980s and could occur again. Drive over to the marina and "check the tires"—a summer breakwater of old tires favored by gulls—for Bonaparte's and Little Gulls, or Caspian and Common Terns. Iceland, Lesser Black-backed, and Glaucous Gulls can also turn up on the bay in winter. Whether trudging through sand or snow, walking on a solid boat ramp, or out on a rocking dock, birders should find Westport and North West Bay rewarding. —**JP**

The Magic Triangle

Drive the rural roads between Westport and Essex, stopping to scan the farm fields for hawks and grassland birds. More than a hundred species nest in the area, and in winter the fields are often visited by Snow Bunting and Bohemian Waxwing.

DIRECTIONS: From the ferry dock in Essex hamlet, drive south on Lake Shore Road about 2.5 miles and turn right onto Whallon's Bay Road (County 55). Go about 2 miles uphill (passing Middle Road on the right) to a crossroads. Here Whallon's Bay Road continues west to Whallonsburg, the Clark Road diverges to the south, and the Cross Road on the extreme left heads east back to Lake Shore Road. Take Clark Road and drive 1.75 miles south to Lake Shore Road, passing Webb Royce Swamp on the left. Take a sharp left on Lake Shore Road and drive north 1.5 miles to Cross Road. Turn left and in a half-mile you'll reach the crossroads again, having driven the perimeter of the Magic Triangle.

Geoffrey Carleton dubbed the triangle of farm roads around the Webb Royce Swamp the Magic Triangle, for the almost supernatural variety of birds found there. More than one hundred species nest in the immediate area, and many more migrants or winter visitants occur. The basic, or lesser, triangle is formed by the Clark, Cross, and Lake Shore roads, with an alternative that extends to include the Whallon's Bay Road. When pressed for details, Jeff Carleton admitted to a Greater Triangle that followed Whallon's Bay Road (County 55) west to Whallonsburg, thence south on Angier Hill Road to the old Angier Hill School, returning north on Lake Shore Road to Whallon's Bay. Birders will discover their own permutations of these basic routes.

Before driving the triangle, it pays to check the waters of Whallon's Bay for waterfowl. From Lake Shore Road, near the turn for Whallon's Bay Road, pull off onto Albee Road, which leads east to the Split Rock lighthouse. Rafts of goldeneye and other diving ducks gather on the bay in winter, and use of a scope may turn up a Barrow's Goldeneye, one of the scoters, loons, or grebes. Scan the shoreline white pines and the sky over Split Rock Point for Bald Eagles in winter. Known to early French settlers as *Rocher fendu*, Split Rock was once the dividing line between French and British territories in North America.

Proceed uphill on Whallon's Bay Road, stopping after a quarter-mile to check the brushy area where a tiny brook crosses for Black-billed Cuckoo in summer or Northern Cardinal in winter. Continue uphill, stopping to scan fields and forests along the road. The fenced-in field on the left, opposite the Middle Road intersection, was planted in winter wheat in the 1970s and plowed in late summer, attracting large flocks of Black-bellied Plover

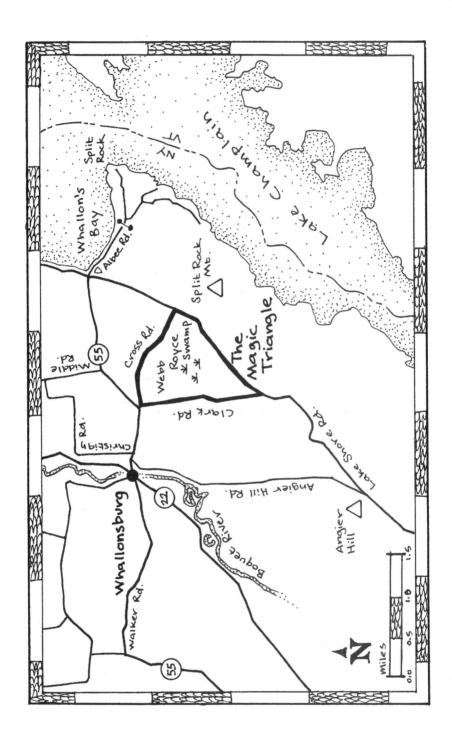

and American Golden-Plover, as well as a Buff-breasted Sandpiper in September 1974. Even a Parasitic Jaeger showed up in the plowed furrows in the wake of Hurricane Frederic in September '79. More recently the fields have been tiled for drainage and planted for hay. Roads of crushed stone and earthen berms have been built as well. This is most apparent from the height of land at the junction of Clark and Cross roads, an area where Short-eared Owl nested and hunted until perhaps 1997. Although the owls appear extirpated from the triangle, the rise above Whallonsburg is still a good vantage point to look for Northern Harrier or Rough-legged Hawk, and the fields are often frequented in winter by Horned Lark and Snow Bunting. Follow Clark Road south, stopping at Webb Royce Swamp and a tiny brook just before reaching Lake Shore Road. In winter, the buckthorn berries in this area often attract large flocks of Bohemian Waxwings. Turn left and follow the shore road to Cross Road, taking another left, checking the wetland at the bottom of the hill for Willow Flycatcher in summer. Having made a circuit, try the Greater Triangle for Vesper Sparrow or Christian and Middle roads to the north for migrant American Pipit. The magical possibilities are endless. **—JP**

Farm fields along Whallon's Bay Road

Photo by Phil Brown

What Happened to Webb Royce Swamp?

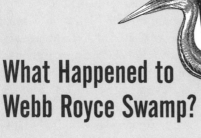

Located within the Magic Triangle, Webb Royce Swamp once was recognized as an Audubon Important Bird Area (IBA), but in the late 1990s, the water level in this hardwood wetland dropped after trappers killed off the beavers, driving away the numerous waterbirds. Birders still pull off at the Clark Road opening to hike along a hedgerow in the vain hope of finding something interesting, but Webb Royce Swamp is best viewed today as a cautionary tale of ecological change and the failure of land stewards to protect significant habitat.

Webb Royce Swamp may have been "the meadows" where settler William Gilliland sent a crew to make hay on July 25, 1765. Winslow C. Watson wrote in 1869, "I cannot determine whether the meadows referred to are the marshes created by the spring overflowing of the low alluvial lands upon the shores of the lake, or those formed by the labors of the beaver, upon streams. I conjecture they were the latter." Over the years, the putative beaver meadow became known as Barnaby Swamp, Black Ash Swamp, Fortune Swamp, and finally Webb Royce Swamp. Webster Royce, who was born in Essex in 1831, owned the swamp and a 410-acre farm and lived in a now-abandoned house along the Clark Road. He also owned the old Essex Inn. One farmhand would cut firewood in the swamp in the fall, and a rattlesnake hunter is said to have worked in the swamp. During a fight with his driver's son, Royce was partially blinded when his opponent rubbed sand in his eyes. Webb was known for his favorite adage, "Don't do today what you can do tomorrow."

By the early 1970s, the swamp was a mature bottomland forest of elm and swamp maple, mud lines on their trunks indicating seasonal flooding of this lens of blue clay, which covers a former glacial lakebed.

The bowl is surrounded by ash, aspen, basswood, hickory, and oak. In the mid-eighties, the aptly named Beaver Brook outlet was dammed by beavers, and over the following decade the newly flooded swamp became home to American Wigeon, Northern Shoveler, Northern Pintail, Green-winged Teal, Ring-necked Duck, Pied-billed Grebe, Great Egret, Black-crowned Night-Heron, Virginia Rail, Common Moorhen, and American Coot. When twenty-one pairs of Great Blue Heron moved north to Four Brothers in 1996, three abandoned nests in the heronry were promptly recycled by pairs of Canada Goose, Osprey, and Great Horned Owl.

New York State, with the help of the Nature Conservancy, later acquired the swamp and allowed in hunters and trappers. At one time, the pool at the southern end could be explored by canoe, or skated on in winter. Soon after the state's purchase, birders found a beaver carcass in the snow. Calls to install a low dam went unheeded, and water levels subsequently dropped in 1997. Now eutrophication is nearly complete and the waterbirds are gone, but one would do well to stop here and reflect for a moment. —**JP**

Photo by Gary Randorf/Adirondack Council

A winter visitor at Webb Royce Swamp

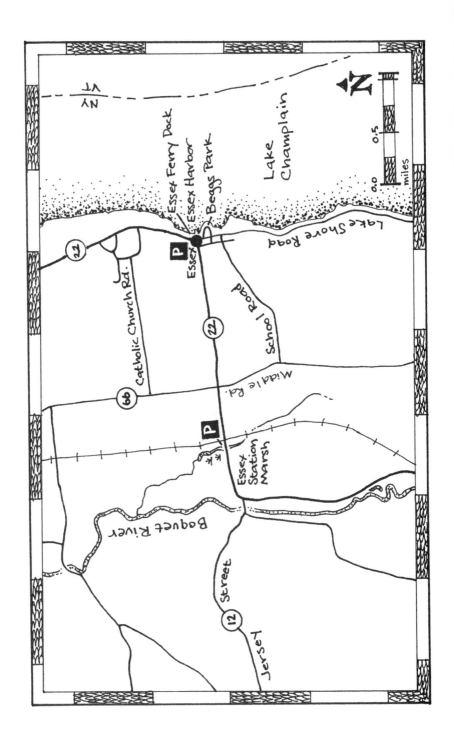

Essex Harbor & Essex Station

Visit the charming hamlet of Essex, whose harbor offers shelter to rafts of waterfowl. Don't be surprised to discover a Barrow's Goldeneye, Ruddy Duck, or other rarity among the flocks. Bald Eagle and four species of gull also frequent the harbor.

DIRECTIONS: From Northway (I-87) Exit 31, go east a few hundred yards, then turn left onto Youngs Road (County 59). Take Youngs Road to its end (about 2.5 miles), turn right onto the Elizabethtown-Wadhams Road (County 8), then make a quick left onto NY 22. Take NY 22 into the hamlet of Essex, about 9.5 miles. At the T intersection, turn left to park in the small public lot opposite the Lake Champlain Transportation Company ferry dock. To reach Essex Station Marsh, drive west on NY 22 from the hamlet to a pull-off near the railroad tracks.

Essex Harbor is most productive outside the summer tourist season, generally from Columbus Day until Memorial Day, except when the harbor and main lake are frozen. This historic hamlet was founded in 1765 by William Gilliland of Armagh, Northern Ireland, who attempted to found a baronial manor, in imitation of those on the Hudson. The Dower House that he presented to his daughter, Elizabeth, and son-in-law, Daniel Ross, on their marriage about 1785 still stands at the north end of the row of houses fronting the harbor. No more charming hamlet can be found on Lake Champlain. Almost all of the lovingly restored houses and buildings date to the heyday of the lake trade in the early nineteenth century.

From the ferry landing, scan the shoreline and harbor north to Sandy Beach, check the area of the pilings and Old Dock House restaurant on the south side, and survey the broad lake toward Charlotte, Vermont, the ferry terminus on the opposite side. Use of a scope is recommended. Depending upon the date and conditions, the resident flock of Mallards may be joined by a variety of other waterfowl species, some quite rare. Look among the more common puddle ducks and abundant goldeneyes and mergansers for a Gadwall, Canvasback, Redhead, Ring-necked Duck, or one of the scaups. An immature drake Harlequin Duck frequented the harbor in January 1986 and a Ruddy Duck in January 2008. The rafts of Common Goldeneye are frequently so close to shore that the landing is an especially rewarding spot to look for a rare Barrow's Goldeneye, not only the distinctive drake, but also a yellow-billed hen. Even a large Western Grebe showed up on New Year's Day 2007. Bald Eagles are regular at the harbor. Four gull species (Bonaparte's, Ring-billed, Herring, and Great Black-backed) occur fairly regularly, with a flock of Ring-billed lingering until the lake freezes, and in midwinter they may be joined by white-winged gulls (Iceland or Glaucous). Modest toilet facilities are available on the dock when the ferry is in operation, but the few local restaurants are generally closed in winter.

From the ferry, walk or drive south past the firehouse, then take either the first or second streets to the left, the entrances to a short loop to Beggs Point Park and a small parking area at the water's edge. The park provides a vista of the main lake and view of the marina to the south, while the street runs past the sheltered little bay on the south side of the Old Dock House, where rarities not visible from the ferry landing may be found. Carefully scan the waves out on the main lake for the tiny periscopes that become Horned Grebes in the scope, or for a dark-gray submarine that reveals itself to be a Common Loon in basic plumage.

If the ferry is running, the fare for a foot passenger to Vermont and back is modest, and the trip affords spectacular views of Lake Champlain, the Adirondacks, and the Green Mountains, and perhaps a string of scoters flying out on the wide lake or other waterfowl gathered in Charlotte Harbor. The round trip takes about an hour, depending on winds and waves. The crossing is a popular one for tourists and skiers, so birders should remain alert for moving vehicles entering and exiting the landing. Even without a rare duck, Essex Harbor is a scenic stop along the lakeshore.

Also worth a visit is Essex Station Marsh on Route 22, one and a half miles west of the hamlet. This modest marsh on both sides of the highway has been a popular stop for birders at least since Geoffrey Carleton found two Baird's Sandpipers here on October 29, 1937, and perhaps even earlier. As

Photo by Phil Brown

The view of Lake Champlain from Beggs Point Park

recently as a quarter-century ago, a variety of other small wetlands and ponds could be found in the town of Essex: marshes at both ends of the Cross Road, Crater Club Pond, two farm ponds on Christian Road outside Whallonsburg, and another below Middle Road near Route 22, but most have eutrophied or been drained or filled. Even Essex Station is less wet than in the past, but the marsh and adjacent abandoned pasture are still productive.

In the past, when the area was seasonally flooded, American Bittern would hunt meadow voles near the water's edge, and when Holsteins were kept in the pasture, they might be joined by a Cattle Egret. Blue-winged Teal nested until at least the 1980s and may still do so, and Green-winged Teal may be present from March to July. The surrounding fields provide a wide vista, so be alert for open-country raptors, such as Turkey Vulture, Red-tailed Hawk, and American Kestrel, and in winter look for a hovering Rough-legged Hawk. An eastern coyote may also be seen working the same fields.

Both Virginia Rail and Sora have nested in the marsh on the south side of the highway, with downy, black Virginia Rail chicks seen from the small highway bridge, emerging from the cattails. Usually, a Sora can be found in flooded grasses and sedges a bit farther back. Common Moorhen was last reported here in May 1954, with none since. Shorebirds are normally seen from the parking area or the north side of the bridge. Look for southbound Semipalmated Plover from late July onward. Greater Yellowlegs may stop in seasonally flooded fields on the south side of Route 22 during late April, while southbound Lesser Yellowlegs occur in the pasture area by early August. Although more expected as a fall migrant, Solitary Sandpiper has occurred in spring. Any "peep" sandpipers are likely to be the more common Semipalmated and Least, but there's always that hidden hope of another Baird's. Displaying Wilson's Snipe often winnow overhead, especially on cloudy days.

From about June 1 until August, you may be able to hear a male Willow Flycatcher singing its sneezy *Fitz-bew!* in the dry brush along the railroad tracks on the south side of the road. Essex Station is one of the few places where both Traill's Flycatchers (the Traill species was split into two, Willow and Alder, in 1973) occur together, with the Alder Flycatcher heard singing *Fee-bee-o* from alders in wetter areas near the marsh. A pair of Sedge Wren frequented the sedges along the tracks in July-August 1995. The habitat remains excellent for this local rarity of grassy marshes and sedgy meadows, so listen for its dry, staccato chattering. If the drying at Essex Station continues, the future of this marsh is uncertain, but for now the site is still worth a visit, and the access is easy. —**JP**

Hawk Lookouts

In spring and fall, many birders head to the hills in the Champlain Valley to watch the migration of hawks and other raptors on their way to and from Canada. More than a dozen species can be observed riding the valley's thermal updrafts, but the most common by far is the Broad-winged Hawk. On a good day, a lucky birder can see dozens of Broad-wingeds passing overhead, usually mingling with other raptors. Broad-wingeds winter in Central and South America. Look for their spring migrations in April and early May and their fall migrations in September and early October. The migration periods of other species vary. The Red-shouldered Hawk, for example, migrates from mid-September to mid-November. Following are three small peaks whose summits offer a scenic perch to look for raptors.

Coon Mountain. Owned by the Adirondack Nature Conservancy. A one-mile trail leads to the summit. From the junction of US 9 and NY 22 in the hamlet of Westport, drive north on NY 22 for a half-mile, turn right on Lakeshore Road, and go about three miles to Halds Road. Turn left and go about a mile to a parking lot on the right.

Belfry Mountain. Perhaps the easiest climb in the Adirondacks. It takes only ten minutes to walk up a gravel road (closed to vehicles) to the fire tower. From Northway (I-87) Exit 30, go south on US 9 for a very short distance, turn left on Tracy Road (County 6), and follow it for about eight miles to Dalton Hill Road (County 7), reached at a four-way junction in the hamlet of Witherbee. Turn left and go about a half-mile north on the Lincoln Pond Road. Look for a yellow gate on the left.

Mount Defiance. A road also leads to the top of this peak, located southwest of Fort Ticonderoga. From Montcalm Street in downtown Ticonderoga, turn south onto the Portage, then take the second left onto Mount Defiance Street. From the gate at the bottom of the hill, you can walk or drive to the summit, listening for Eastern Towhee in the oak woods. The gate is closed at night. Migrant raptors often make the Lake George-Lake Champlain transition at Mount Defiance, lifted by thermals from South Mountain.

Illustration by Mike Storey

6 Noblewood Park

Walk to a bluff overlooking Lake Champlain and through a bottomland forest to the sandy mouth of the Boquet River. Depending on the habitat and season, you may see anything from Red-throated Loon to Black-headed Gull to Red-bellied Woodpecker.

DIRECTIONS: From Essex hamlet, follow NY 22 north toward Willsboro. After 3 miles, rounding a curve to the left, look for the Noblewood Park sign and driveway on the right. From Willsboro, follow NY 22 toward Essex and look for the Noblewood sign on the left, just past Memorial and Calvary cemeteries. There may be an entrance fee. Pedestrian access is free when the park is not open.

Located on the south bank of the Boquet River delta, this sixty-four-acre park quickly became one of the most popular birding destinations along Lake Champlain after the town of Willsboro acquired the property in the late 1990s. Before then, the delta could be accessed only by boat, since both banks at the mouth of the river were privately owned. With help from the Adirondack Nature Conservancy and the Paine family, the town obtained grants to purchase the land for two hundred thousand dollars. At the time, Willsboro Supervisor (later Assemblywoman) Teresa Sayward noted that the town contained twenty-one miles of lakefront but only 250 feet with public access. Birders are not the only beneficiaries of her vision in creating Noblewood Park, which opened to the public in 1999.

Walk through the pedestrian opening at the side of the gate, and in twenty yards you'll come to a fork in the road. The road to the right leads to a bluff overlooking the lake and the shoreline to the south, with steep steps leading down to park buildings just south of the beach. The bluff offers views of waterfowl not always visible from below and is well worth checking out, especially in winter. Scope any geese and diving ducks for a Redhead, one of the scoters, Long-tailed Duck, Barrow's Goldeneye, Red-throated Loon, or Red-necked Grebe. Continuing on the entrance road, you soon come to a parking area on the right, where another road descends through a mixed woods that transitions from locust to hemlock to bottomland forest. Red-bellied Woodpecker, Yellow-bellied and Willow Flycatchers, Yellow-throated and Philadelphia Vireos, and Bay-breasted and Blackpoll Warblers have been found along the trail and shoreline. Other trails branch off at the bottom. Bear left to the canoe launch on the river, the trail favored by birders. (Another trail to the right, sometimes seasonally flooded, leads to the lake and past the state's largest pitch pine among the pines on the left.) Take a right at the river, walking east through the sand to the

Mouth of the Boquet River

Photo by Susan Bibeau

Boquet delta. Barrels of the fine black sand underfoot were once shipped to cities for use in sand shakers, essential nineteenth-century desktop items in the days of quill and steel pens. The sand was used to dry ink on rag paper. Colonial waterbirds from the **Four Brothers Islands** gather along the shore in summer: Double-crested Cormorant, Great Blue Heron, Great Egret, Black-crowned Night-Heron, Ring-billed, Herring, and Great Black-backed Gulls, and Caspian Tern, joined by up to a thousand migrant Bonaparte's Gull, several hundred Common Tern, a few Black Tern and Little Gull, and an occasional Black-headed Gull. Scan the beaches for any of twenty species of shorebirds. Noblewood has had Whimbrel (May and August 2004, maximum seven), Red Knot (September '03, August '04, maximum, five), Western Sandpiper (August '03 and '07), Stilt Sandpiper (August '07), Red-necked Phalarope (August '04), Baird's Sandpiper (most summers), and American Golden-Plover (rare). In fall, the beaches also attract American Pipit and Snow Bunting, the latter lingering into winter. A wayward hen Tufted Duck showed up on November 7, 2007, but even without rarities, Noblewood Park is a lovely spot for a quiet walk. —**JP**

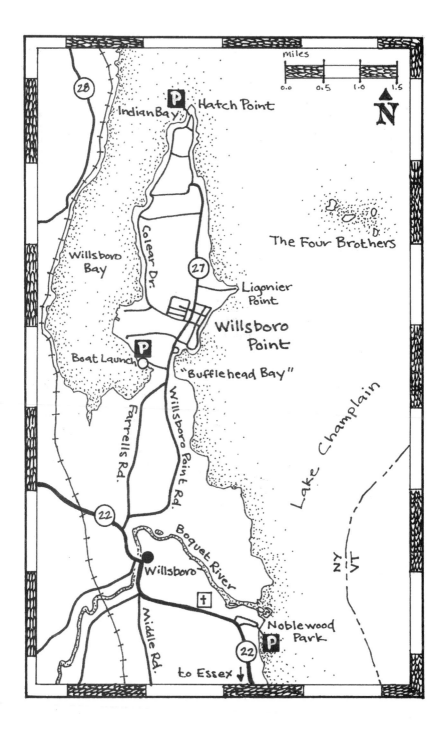

miles

0.0   0.5   1.0   1.5

N

28

Hatch Point

Indian Bay

Colear Dr.

27

The Four Brothers

Willsboro Bay

Ligonier Point

Willsboro Point

Boat Launch

"Bufflehead Bay"

Farrells Rd.

Willsboro Point Rd.

Lake Champlain

22

Boquet River

Willsboro

NY VT

Middle Rd.

Noblewood Park

22

to Essex ↓

Bent cedars at Hatch Point

7 Willsboro Point

Look for Snow Bunting, Horned Lark, and Eastern Bluebird in the fields of this large peninsula on Lake Champlain, then scan the lake and Willsboro Bay for Bufflehead, loons, mergansers, gulls, and a variety of puddle and diving ducks.

DIRECTIONS: From the Boquet River bridge in Willsboro hamlet, follow NY 22 uphill to the west (toward Long Pond and I-87). At the top of the rise, turn right onto Farrell Road (County 27B). Shortly after the turn, there is an intersection with Willsboro Point Road (County 27) on the right. You can take either road, since they rejoin after a few miles, but Farrell Road is more direct. After they rejoin, continue north (now on Willsboro Point Road) for 0.2 miles and then turn left onto the access road to the Willsboro Bay Boat Launch, marked by a DEC sign. See map, p. 45

Willsboro Point is a four-mile peninsula extending northward into Lake Champlain, with Willsboro Bay to the west and the main lake to the east. The northern tip affords a view of the main lake north to Schuyler Island and east to Four Brothers Islands. The habitat is largely a mix of open fields and abandoned farmlands now grown into brush and early second-growth forests. Structures vary from nineteenth-century stone mansions to trailer parks, old barns to modern marinas. Birding is best in winter before the bay freezes, when the smaller coves provide shelter for a wide variety of waterfowl.

If the Farrell Road flats are snow-covered, watch the open fields and road shoulders for flocks of Snow Buntings or Horned Larks, sometimes accompanied by unobtrusive Lapland Longspurs in dingy winter plumage. At the DEC sign for the boat launch, take the access road straight ahead to a large parking lot and boat ramp at a bay on the south end of Willsboro Bay. The bay at the launch has a variety of puddle ducks, diving ducks, and mergansers until ice forms, and a Double-crested Cormorant may linger into January. Even if the bay is frozen, check flocks of gulls on the ice; a Glaucous Gull in first-winter plumage was seen in early January 2004. Walk over to the high bank just to the west and scan the shoreline of the bay toward Willsboro Bay Marina for a White-winged or Black Scoter, or any other ducks not visible from the parking lot.

Drive back out the access road, turn left on Willsboro Point Road, then take an almost immediate right onto a side road. Pull off where the road swings left and check the small bay on the lake side. Birders know this as Bufflehead Bay for the attractive divers that favor it, but a wide variety of waterfowl may be found. Scan

Snow Bunting

Illustration by Mike Storey

the waters of the main lake with a scope for Horned Grebes and loons. Continue on the side road, which loops back to Willsboro Point Road. Eastern Bluebirds may be found in winter near the Buena Vista trailer park; they were joined in January 2000 by a brilliant Pine Warbler. Continue north on Willsboro Point Road for about three more miles to the tip of the peninsula at Hatch Point. Park here and take the short trail through cedar-oak woods out to the tip (it's a two-minute walk). Scan the broad waters of the lake north to Schuyler Island for loons. In May 1982, during a return flight of Boreal Chickadees, a flock hovered over the oaks of Hatch Point, reluctant to cross the open water. Tufted Titmice and House Finches are more likely to be found here, especially in winter. From Hatch Point the road heads back to the south past Indian Bay, on the western shore of the peninsula. Stop at any of the numerous coves along the Willsboro Bay side and scan the pines and cliffs across the bay for Bald Eagles. After passing the marina at Indian Bay, the road swings east to rejoin Willsboro Point Road, north of the boat launch. By then, an impressive list of waterfowl should have been seen around Willsboro Point. —JP

Photo by J.M.C. Peterson

Ring-billed Gulls over Lake Champlain

8 Four Brothers Islands

Pick a calm day to paddle to this sanctuary for colonial waterbirds. Among the species that nest are Black-crowned Night-Heron, Cattle Egret, Glossy Ibis, Caspian Tern, and Double-crested Cormorant. Snowy Egret and Common Tern also have been observed.

DIRECTIONS: Owned since 1992 by the Nature Conservancy, these four Lake Champlain islands (totaling just 17.8 acres) are located 5 miles north-northeast of Noblewood Park and 2 miles east of Willsboro Point. The Four Brothers are home to the largest and most diverse waterbird colonies on the lake, but they are accessible only by boat, either from the state boat launch at the foot of Willsboro Bay (a 7-mile trip, one way) or a local marina. Extreme caution is advised, especially in sailboats or sea kayaks. As the conservancy signs advise, "Please look, but do not land." See map, p. 45.

The Four Brothers are shale islands, covered with a mantle of glacial till, in the middle of Lake Champlain. Originally, they supported a rich diversity of woodland plants under ash, elm, and basswood trees. Today, most of the plants are European, not native, and the abundance of species with prickles, spines, and thorns suggests past grazing by domesticated animals that devoured the less-armored flora. The French knew the islands as Les Iles des Quatre Vents, or the Islands of the Four Winds. In the mid-eighteenth century, Swedish naturalist Pehr (Peter) Kalm passed the islands twice on his trip to Montréal, even taking refuge from a storm in Willsboro Bay during his return, but he made no mention of the birds. About 1850, the Reverend G. Ingersoll collected Herring Gull eggs on "one of the islands called Four Brothers." For another century, this was the only colonial species that nested. Alvah Jordan visited the islands with Augustus Paine in May 1887 to collect adult gulls and eggs where a large colony existed a decade before, "but owing to the relentless persecution of the farmers and small boys, who gathered their eggs by the basketfull [sic], the colony had been reduced to some fifty pairs, and I do not think they raised a single brood last season." After ownership passed from the Shipman family to the Hatches about 1892, Edward Hatch began hiring wardens to guard the colony in summer out of his fondness for the gulls, providing a cabin (foundation stones and a rusted bedspring mark the spot today), motorboat, food and clothing, guns and fishing tackle, and even books. Army Lt. L.R. Wolfe rowed with Edward's son, Livingston Hatch, on May 22, 1922, to the island nearest Willsboro Point, "covered with an open growth of scrub pine, juniper and a scant covering of grass," finding fifty-two gull nests and "an old and dilapidated shack and several chicken coops."

Bird banding commenced in June 1925, with Herring Gull recoveries from as far away as Veracruz, Mexico, and the Pacific coast of Guatemala. Ring-billed Gull arrived in 1949. The Ring-bills expanded to 17,347 nests by 1983, but they went into serious decline after the closing of the region's open landfills (one of the banded gulls ended up in Donegal, Ireland). A state biologist from Vermont visited the northeast island in May 1951, "removed one Black-crowned Night-Heron egg and blew it" (after making holes in each end). Since that time, banded night-herons from here have been shot as far away as Yablis, Nicaragua, and the island of Terceira in the Azores. Cattle Egrets have nested sporadically since 1974, and Great Black-backed Gulls arrived in 1975, with a few pairs now on each island. Double-crested Cormorants first arrived in 1951 and began nesting in 1984, soon joined by a variety of other colonial waterbirds: Great Blue Heron (1993), Glossy Ibis (1999), Great Egret (2000), and Caspian Tern (2004). Snowy Egret and Common Tern are often present but not yet proven to nest.

In the twentieth century, the Hatches sold the islands to John Astor. Ownership later passed to the University of Vermont and finally in 1992 to the Nature Conservancy. The Audubon Society managed the islands for twenty-one years, until 2003. Vermont biologists have assigned letter names to the islands, in order of their proximity to Burlington: Island A (2.3 acres) in the northeast, Island B (2.4 acres) to the southeast, Island C (6.9 acres), the large central plateau, and Island D (6.2 acres), the one nearest the New York shore. The Four Brothers are home to birds that roam far across the Atlantic and into the Pacific, and they deserve our study and protection. **—JP**

Island A of the Four Brothers

Port Kent & Wickham Marsh

Go to the marsh in spring or summer to look for nesting Blue-winged Teal, Common Goldeneye, Virginia Rail, and Common Moorhen. Listen for Yellow-throated Vireo in the adjacent woods. Walk across the road to observe waterfowl on Lake Champlain.

DIRECTIONS: From the north side of the NY 9 bridge over Ausable Chasm, take NY 373 about 3 miles east to the Port Kent Amtrak shelter. Proceed across the railroad tracks downhill to the ferry landing, then return and take Lake Street to the right, through the hamlet, and continue 2 miles on Lakeside Road to the Wickham Marsh Wildlife Management Area, marked by a DEC sign on the left side. Continue north on Lakeside Road and follow the curve to the left to reach a viewing platform. See map, p. 54.

While not all visitors to Port Kent and Wickham Marsh will be fortunate enough to find a Tufted Duck or Western Grebe, the possibilities of such rarities make this a popular site for watching waterfowl. In 2007, the state Department of Environmental Conservation constructed a viewing platform near the marsh as a tribute to the late Geoffrey Carleton. Use of a spotting scope here is highly recommended.

In Port Kent, park at the Amtrak station and from the top of the high bank across the tracks scan Lake Champlain and the shoreline to the south, as far as Trembleau Point. Common Goldeneyes, Common Mergansers, and other divers congregate here from fall until the lake freezes in winter. Drive down to the ferry landing's parking lot, scan the shoreline to the north, where American Black Ducks and Mallards often gather, and check around the pilings of the dock for Ring-necked Duck, White-winged Scoter, or other ducks. Great Black-backed Gulls are regular, and Bonaparte's and Glaucous occur. A rare Western Grebe was found here in November 2005 and again in October and December 2006, a wanderer from the far side of the continent.

Returning to the top of the hill, take a right on Lake Street to drive through Port Kent hamlet and north toward Wickham Marsh. In January 2003, a drake Tufted Duck from Eurasia was picked out of a large raft of a thousand Greater Scaup from the bluff just outside the hamlet. Continue two miles, checking the lake for waterfowl, and park in the small DEC lot on the left at the entrance to Wickham Marsh Wildlife Management Area. From the railroad embankment across the road, scan the main lake north to Ausable Beach, where Bald Eagles often stand on the ice shelf as the lake freezes. Carefully checking the large flocks of Common Goldeneyes that frequent this area may reward persistence with a rare Barrow's Goldeneye. The large rafts of over a thousand Canvasback that gathered here in the

1970s are now sadly a thing of the past, but other waterfowl–notably gold-eneyes and mergansers–still occur in the thousands into January or later when the lake is open. Up to six Ruddy Ducks and as many as twenty Red-throated Loons have also been recorded here during November.

Wickham Marsh itself is equally rewarding in spring and summer. Nesting waterbirds include Blue-winged Teal, Common Goldeneye, Virginia Rail, and Common Moorhen. Again, a scope is suggested. Listen in the rich bottomland hardwoods along the start of the trail for the burry *ee-yay, three-eight* song of the regionally rare Yellow-throated Vireo. The trail continues for 0.3 miles through the woods and out into the open, with the marsh on the right, before ending. Views of the marsh are not rewarding, but rails and northern birds can sometimes be heard, and Marsh Wrens and Swamp Sparrows frequent the edges. Just north of the DEC parking area and the marsh, Lakeside Road curves west, becoming Back Road, and leads to another parking area on the left. A short trail leads to the Carleton viewing platform overlooking the marsh from a high vantage.

For sheer numbers of winter waterfowl, Wickham Marsh is one of the premier spots on Lake Champlain. You can return to Route 9 by continuing on the Back Road or taking the Plains Road, a right fork. **—JP**

Wickham Marsh

⑩ Ausable Point

Set up a scope on a platform that extends into a marsh teeming with waterfowl, including Wood Duck, Great Egret, and American Bittern. Across the road, look for Ring-necked Duck, Redhead, and other diving ducks on Lake Champlain.

DIRECTIONS: From Northway (I-87) Exit 32, drive east on NY 442 about 3 miles to US 9. Turn left and go 0.4 miles to the state campground entrance road on the right, marked by a DEC sign. Follow the entrance road as far as the tollbooth or to the campground and beach beyond.

Ausable Point combines ease of access with some superb birding habitat. Surrounded by Lake Champlain on the north and east, this delta area between the Little Ausable River and upper mouth of the Ausable River features wetlands and shoreline that are part of the Ausable Marsh Wildlife Management Area and the adjacent state campground and beach. The first half-mile of the access road, bordered by the lake and marshes, can provide a variety of waterfowl and other birds in all seasons. Birders generally don't venture beyond this first stretch when the campground tollbooth beyond is open. In summer, when the campground and beach are in operation, go early in the morning to avoid the traffic and the toll.

A short way down the access road, stop near the bridge over the Little Ausable and check for Wood Duck, Blue-winged Teal, Hooded Merganser, and other waterfowl. Continue along the road, stopping to check the lake on the left for diving ducks, especially in winter: Canvasback, Redhead, Ring-necked Duck, large rafts of both scaup, all three scoters, Long-tailed Duck, Bufflehead, and both goldeneyes. Even Cackling Goose, Eurasian Wigeon, and Tufted Duck were spotted in late March 2007. Listen for Virginia Rail and Common Moorhen, and watch for American Coot. If Bonaparte's Gulls are present, be alert for a Little Gull among them. Check the nest atop a power pole on the right, or Osprey platform farther along, for signs of occupancy. Stop and scan the marshes and pools on the right side of the road for puddle ducks, American Bittern, Great Blue Heron, and Great Egret. Look and listen for rails. Watch the mudflats around emergent clumps of vegetation for Wilson's Snipe, or listen for

Photo by John Thaxton

Black-crowned Night-Heron chicks

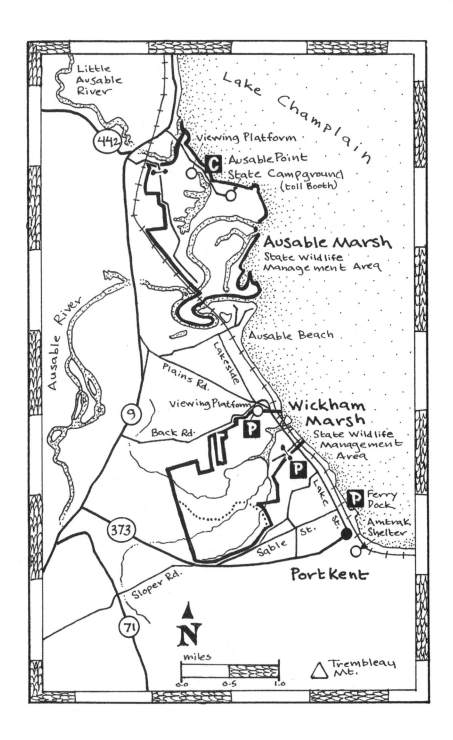

Little
Ausable
River

Lake Champlain

442

Viewing Platform

C Ausable Point
State Campground
(toll Booth)

Ausable Marsh
State Wildlife
Management Area

Ausable River

Ausable Beach

Lakeside

Plains Rd.

9

Viewing Platform

P

Back Rd.

Wickham
Marsh
State Wildlife
Management
Area

P

Lake St.

P Ferry
Dock

Amtrak
Shelter

373

Sable St.

Port Kent

Sloper Rd.

71

N

miles
0.0   0.5   1.0

△ Trembleau
Mt.

Photo by Carl Heilman II

Ausable Marsh

their winnowing overhead. Watch the wires and air overhead for all five species of swallow found in the region. Although the marsh is normally frozen by December, the lake may remain open until January or beyond, with the number and variety of diving ducks increasing as Champlain freezes over from the north and south. Stop at the viewing platform, a memorial to naturalist Greenleaf ("Greenie") Chase, just before the bridge over the channel. The platform doesn't provide much of an elevated view, but it extends into the marsh and provides a stable setting for spotting scopes. The channel is suitable for launching a canoe or kayak to paddle along the lakeshore around Ausable Point, past the beach and campground, to the upper mouth of the Ausable River delta. When launching, watch out for the monofilament lines of fishermen who gather here, and use caution if the lake is rough.

The parking area near the tollbooth and brushy areas beyond hosted a rare Yellow-throated Warbler from mid-November 2006 until late January 2007, and the woods and bushes past the tollbooth host a variety of warblers. A mix of shorebirds rest and feed on the beaches and delta in late summer and fall, and Bald Eagles are regular in winter. Other possibilities range from Snowy Owl to Blue-gray Gnatcatcher, and new finds are always being made at Ausable Point. **—JP**

Chazy Riverlands

Make a pilgrimage to the pasturelands that have attracted more rare birds than any other site in the Champlain Valley: Ross's Goose, Eurasian Wigeon, Arctic Tern, and Stilt Sandpiper, to name a few. The fields can be observed from the road or from Lake Champlain.

DIRECTIONS: From Adirondack Northway (I-87) Exit 41, follow County 191 east for 0.9 miles to NY 9, turn right, go 0.4 miles to Church Street, and turn left. The road soon forks; take the left tine onto North Farm Road and continue 2.4 miles to the T-intersection with Lake Shore Road. Turn left, crossing the Little Chazy River at 0.6 miles, and continue 2 miles north on Lake Shore Road to Laventure Drive, the access road for the DEC boat launch at the mouth of the Great Chazy River.

These riverlands, bounded by the two Chazy Rivers, are perhaps the premier birding area of the Adirondack-Champlain region. No other site has produced as many avian rarities in recent decades. Access is something of a problem, since most of the lakeshore corridor is private land with numerous fenced fields, often occupied by grazing Holsteins. Starting at a farm with many silos at North Farm Road, drive almost three miles north on Lake Shore Road, stopping to scan the fields on both sides, especially when seasonally flooded in spring, for geese, ducks, and grassland birds. A Glossy Ibis was wading here on April 21, 1993. Check the vicinity of the

Holsteins at the Laurin Farm

Photo by Phil Brown

Boreal Chickadee

Plate 1

American Bittern

Virginia Rail

Wood Duck

Ring-necked Duck

Plate 2

Northern Harrier

Northern Parula

Savannah Sparrow

Bobolink

Plate 3

Bonaparte's Gull

Pectoral Sandpiper

Plate 4

Blue-headed Vireo

Philadelphia Vireo

Red-eyed Vireo

Plate 5

Bohemian Waxwing

Rough-legged Hawk

Snow Bunting

Short-eared Owl

Plate 6

Blackpoll Warbler

Mourning Warbler

Blackburnian Warbler

Pine Warbler

Plate 7

Scarlet Tanager

Barred Owl

Hermit Thrush

Ovenbird

Plate 8

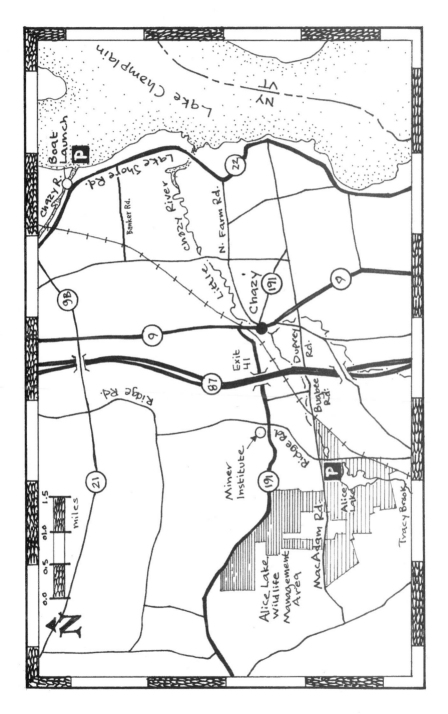

Lake Champlain

NY / VT

Boat Launch

Chazy R.

Lake Shore Rd.

Chazy River

Banker Rd.

N. Farm Rd.

22

Little

Chazy

191

9

9B

Exit 41

87

Dupee Rd.

Bupbee Rd.

Ridge Rd.

21

Ridge Rd.

Miner Institute

191

MacAdam Rd.

Alice Lake Wildlife Management Area

Alice Lake

Tracy Brook

miles
0.0 0.5 0.6 0.6 1.5

N

bridge over the Little Chazy and continue birding slowly northward toward the state boat launch at the mouth of the Great Chazy. After Banker Road enters on the left, pay careful attention to the pastures on the right and the vast fields to the left. Large flocks of Snow and Canada Geese feed in the fields during migration, and both Snowy and Short-eared Owls may be found in winter, the latter near dusk (eight were seen in February 1995). Winter may also bring flocks of Horned Lark, Lapland Longspur, and Snow Bunting. Park at the boat launch and check the mouth of the Great Chazy. The best way to view the marshy shoreline and fields to the south is to launch a canoe or kayak here. From the ramp, paddle to the right, following the shoreline to the south a half-mile or more. About a hundred yards north of a large pile of fieldstones near the lakeshore, look for an opening in the cattails and rushes, then a shallow pool in the pasture beyond. This is the famed Laurin Farm, adjacent to the equally famous Gravelle Farm.

The rarities found in the Chazy Riverlands since the 1960s, most of them in the vicinity of these neighboring farms, defies credulity. Fortunate birders have found Ross's Goose (April 1995), Tundra Swan (April '79, May '96), Eurasian Wigeon (April '77, but now almost annual in spring), Cinnamon Teal (September '98), Northern Gannet (October '98), Snowy Egret (several times, as recently as September '06), Glossy Ibis (July '01), Golden Eagle (May '07), American Avocet (September '98), Little Gull (most recently May '07), Black-headed Gull (September '07), Caspian Tern (first in May '82, increasingly common), Arctic Tern (May '99 and '04), and Forster's Tern (July '07). A drake Ruddy Duck in July '07 was suspected of nesting. At least twenty-one species of shorebirds occur, including Willet (September '92, June '93, May '03), Hudsonian Godwit (October '77, June '93, May '97), Marbled Godwit (August '94, August '07), Western Sandpiper (regular since May '62), Stilt Sandpiper (August-September '96, July-August '06, August '07), Buff-breasted Sandpiper (September '06), Ruff (more properly Reeves, September '94 and May '05), and both Short-billed and Long-billed Dowitchers. First found at Chazy Riverlands in May 1981, Wilson's Phalarope was confirmed as nesting in New York State for the first time in 1993, with a pair present May 18 and the male seen with three chicks on June 18; breeding has occurred or been attempted several years since. A singing male Nelson's Sharp-tailed Sparrow found in late July 2002 was also suspected of nesting. Even a bird believed to be an Eastern Yellow Wagtail was seen by a single observer at Laurin Farm on September 13, 2005. These are but a few of the reasons to plan a pilgrimage to the Chazy Riverlands. —**JP**

12 Lake Alice

Hike through fields and woods, keeping an eye and ear out for the hundred or so species that nest in this wildlife-management area, including Red-headed Woodpecker, Yellow-throated Vireo, and Northern Waterthrush.

DIRECTIONS: From Exit 41 of the Northway (I-87), take County 191 less than a mile west to the Miner Agricultural Research Institute and turn left onto Ridge Road. Drive south on Ridge Road, crossing McAdam (also called Duprey) Road after a mile. Go another 0.3 miles on Ridge Road and look for the parking lot of the Lake Alice Wildlife Management Area on the right. The entrance is flanked by rocks. See map, p. 57.

The 650-acre area around Lake Alice, named for the wife of former owner William H. Miner Jr., became a state Wildlife Management Area in July 1953. There is a variety of habitat here besides the lake itself, including woods, fields, and marshes, so it's no surprise that as many as a hundred species of birds breed here in summer.

From the parking lot, listen for Warbling Vireo and American Redstart in the surrounding trees or Eastern Meadowlark singing in the fields. The main trail is a wide path that starts at a vehicle barrier to the left of the lot, but there also is a pair of secondary trails leading into the WMA. One is a narrow path that cuts through the woods. Look for it on the right side of the lot. The other trail begins farther to the right and follows the edge of the woods along the outlet of Lake Alice.

To see the greatest variety of habitat, start on one of the secondary trails. The two merge after about seventy-five yards and thus can be combined into a short loop, where flycatchers, vireos, thrushes, and warblers frequent the

A bay of Lake Alice

Photo by Phil Brown

woods and waterbirds gather on the outlet. After the merger, the trail crosses the lake's outlet on a wooden bridge, with marshy stillwaters on either side, and then winds along the edge of an old orchard to join the main route about a quarter-mile from the lot. You can turn left here to return to the lot, completing a somewhat longer loop, or turn right to walk deeper into the WMA. The main trail more or less parallels the marshy lakeshore, passing through fields and deciduous woods. In one clearing, a short path on the right leads to two wetlands. The main trail forks about a half-mile from the lot, with the left tine continuing along the shore and the right veering into the forest.

Depending upon the season, the marshes along the lake and the outlet might have a variety of migrant waterfowl or breeding marsh birds such as Green Heron, Virginia Rail, Sora, and Marsh Wren. Listen for American Bittern pumping in the reeds in late spring or in summer. During migration, the lake may be covered with Snow Geese or other waterfowl.

Look and listen for Baltimore Oriole among the trees along the lake. The woods anywhere along the route have a variety of woodpeckers, including Yellow-bellied Sapsucker and Pileated, and a Red-headed Woodpecker is always a possibility (one was found here as recently as July 2004). Inside the forest search for Great Crested Flycatcher, Yellow-throated Vireo, Rose-breasted Grosbeak, and woodland warblers (Black-throated Blue, Black-throated Green, Ovenbird, and others). Northern Waterthrush frequent wet areas. If you go as far as the fork and continue along the lake, look for Spotted Sandpiper. A Bald Eagle was seen perched along the shore here in 2007.

McAdam (or Duprey) Road skirts the north end of the lake and is also worth a visit. The woods have nesting Broad-winged and Red-shouldered Hawks and Barred Owl, and birders should again be alert for Red-headed Woodpecker or Yellow-throated Vireo. Since being found here in 1981, Golden-winged Warbler has also occurred in the vicinity. Birders should use caution during hunting seasons (including spring turkey season), staying on the road and not straying into the woods. **—JP**

High Peaks Region

Feathered Friends in High Places

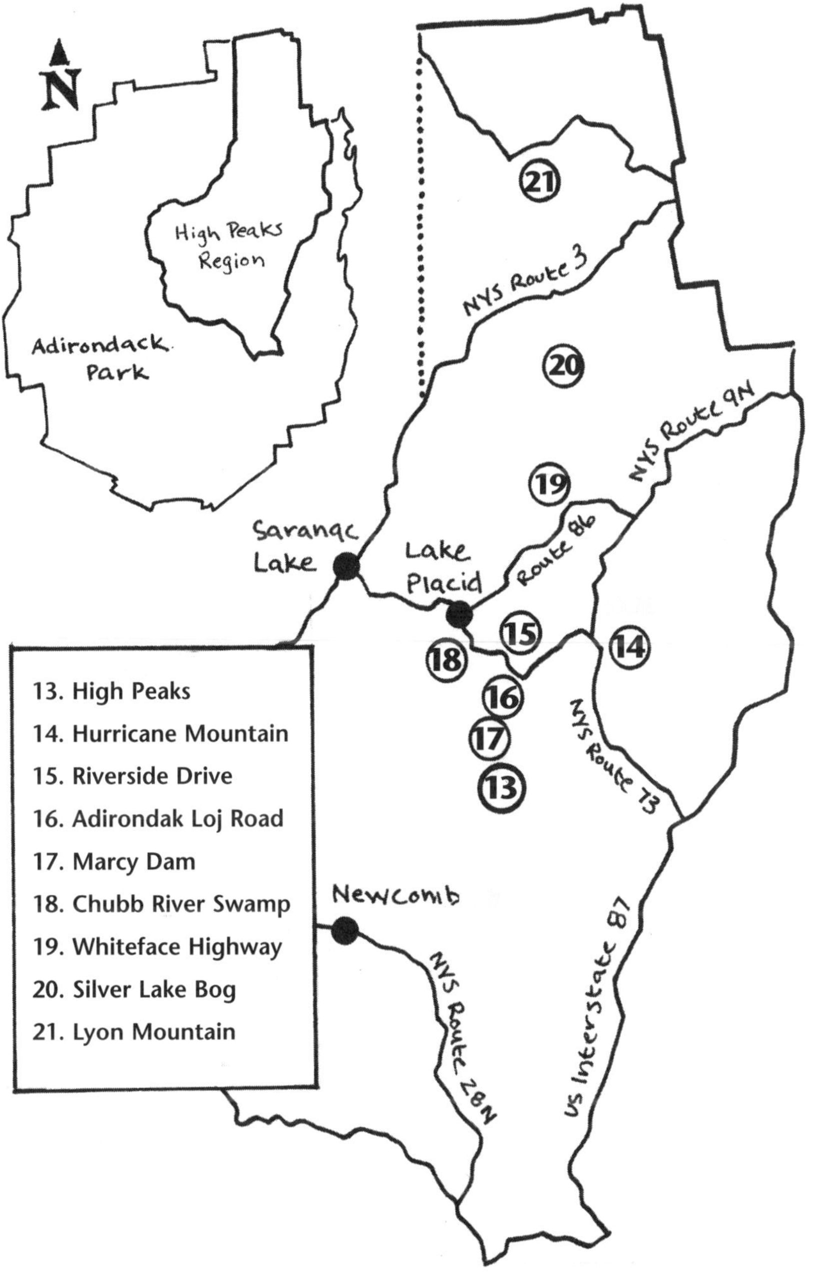
N
High Peaks Region
Adirondack Park
21
NYS Route 3
20
NYS Route 9N
19
Saranac Lake
Lake Placid
Route 86
15
14
18
16
17
13
NYS Route 73
Newcomb
NYS Route 28N
US Interstate 87
13. High Peaks
14. Hurricane Mountain
15. Riverside Drive
16. Adirondak Loj Road
17. Marcy Dam
18. Chubb River Swamp
19. Whiteface Highway
20. Silver Lake Bog
21. Lyon Mountain

View of the High Peaks from the Three Brothers in Keene Valley

Photo by Carl Heilman II

⑬ High Peaks

Ascend one or more of the state's tallest mountains to find boreal species such as Black-backed Woodpecker, Philadelphia Vireo, and Boreal Chickadee. Even if you don't find good birds, the views from up high will reward your effort.

DIRECTIONS: The major trailheads for the High Peaks are at Adirondak Loj, Elk Lake, the Garden (Keene Valley), and Tahawus. See accompanying map for locations. There are a number of less-used trailheads as well. Consult *Adirondack Trails: High Peaks Region* and its accompanying topographical map, published by the Adirondack Mountain Club. The National Geographic map "Adirondack Park: Lake Placid/High Peaks" is another good resource. Be sure to sign in at trail registers, dress appropriately, and be prepared for inclement conditions.

The High Peaks rise as high as the 5,344-foot summit of Mount Marcy, but the number of avian species declines as tree line is reached, and so experienced birders often confine their searches to lower elevations. Many trails give access to the mountains, but see **Marcy Dam** for one popular route. More than a hundred species of breeding birds occur, with boreal species a highlight. Migrants and winter visitants add to the list of possibilities.

Spruce Grouse are extremely rare but Ruffed Grouse common on the trails. Raptors are frequently seen from the summits, especially during spring and fall migration, and may include Golden Eagle and Peregrine Falcon. Along forested trails, only a glimpse of an accipiter can be expected, although the state's first breeding record of Merlin in modern times was provided by a newly fledged falcon along the Cascade Mountain trail in July 1985. The common owls are Barred and Northern Saw-whet, but an elusive Long-eared Owl may also be heard calling at night, especially around montane bodies of water such as Round Pond on the trail to Dix Mountain. Listen for any soft tapping, as the chance of encountering a Black-backed Woodpecker is strong. In shady boreal conifers, listen for Yellow-bellied Flycatcher. The *killink* song is similar to that of a Least Flycatcher, the *tu-wee* call reminiscent of Eastern Wood-Pewee, and the *brrrrt* disturbed territorial call something like the note of an Eastern Phoebe, all birds unlikely to be found in spruce-balsam forest. Those familiar with vireo songs may find a Philadelphia Vireo in medium-height, second-growth deciduous woods, such as Scott Clearing or the Upper Works. Gray Jays have been known to eat out of the hands of backcountry skiers high on Marcy. Gray Jays also have been spotted on Allen Mountain, in Panther Gorge, and at other locales, but such sightings are rare. Common Raven and Boreal Chickadee should be expected, however.

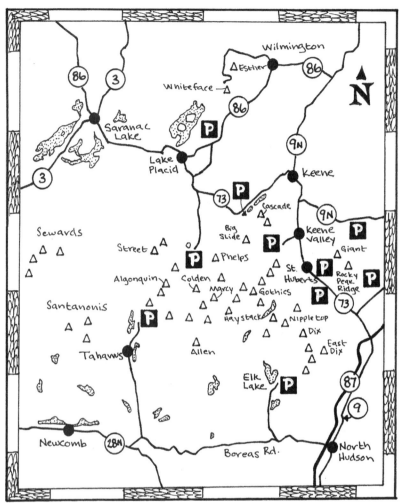

The major High Peaks trailheads

A wayward Northern Wheatear was found above tree line on 4,960-foot Mount Haystack on May 27, 2006. The sought-after Bicknell's Thrush is present near almost all the high summits and may be found as low as Lake Colden, at 2,750 feet. During 2007, Mountain Birdwatch volunteers found more than eighty singing Bicknell's males on twenty-two mountains. These included the following High Peaks (those above four thousand feet): Big Slide, Colden, Esther, Giant, Gothics, Marcy, Phelps, Porter, **Whiteface**, and Wright. In addition, they were found on a number of mountains that fall a little short of four thousand feet (many located far from the High Peaks region): Ampersand, Blue, Gore, Little Whiteface, **Lyon**, McKenzie, Noonmark, **Pillsbury**, Pitchoff, Snowy, Sunrise, and **Wakely**. American Pipits have been found in fall migration (September-October) on the summits of Cascade, East Dix, Gothics, Marcy, Noonmark, Rocky Peak Ridge, Skylight, and Whiteface, the alpine zone resembling the tundra where they nest. Warblers include spruce-budworm specialists such as Tennessee, Cape May, Bay-breasted, and Blackpoll; the last is especially abundant as higher elevations are reached, the males proclaiming territories with a thin, high *zi-zi-zi-zi-zi-zi-zi-zi* song. Listen for the rich Purple Finch-like song of Lincoln's Sparrow, or its agitated *tink*! call in boggy areas. In winters with a bumper cone crop, both Red and White-winged Crossbills nest in the High Peaks, seemingly oblivious to the cold, their rich songs and loud call notes ringing through the snowy forests. These are but a few of the birds waiting to greet hikers, snowshoers, or cross-country skiers. **—JP**

Photo by Jeff Nadler

Common Raven

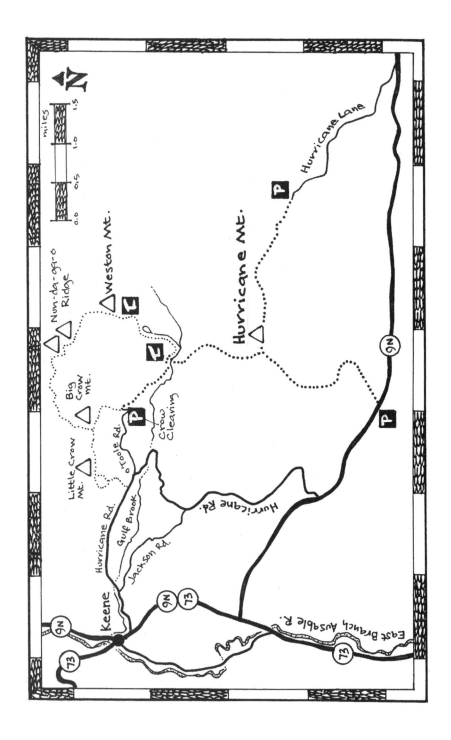

14 Hurricane Mountain

If you climb this popular peak on a nice day, you're sure to enjoy a spectacular view, and if you're lucky, you'll share the summit with a Bicknell's Thrush. Boreal Chickadee and Philadelphia Vireo also have been found on Hurricane.

DIRECTIONS: Three trails lead to the summit of Hurricane Mountain and its closed fire tower. **East trailhead:** From the intersection of US 9 and NY 9N in Elizabethtown, take 9N west for 2.2 miles and turn right onto Hurricane Mountain Lane. Take the steep uphill grade another 2.7 miles to a gate and small parking area on the right. **South trailhead:** From Elizabethtown, continue driving west on NY 9N for 4.5 miles past Hurricane Mountain Lane to a parking lot on the left. From Keene, the lot is 3.5 miles east of NY 73. **North trailhead:** From Keene hamlet, turn off NY 73 onto Hurricane Road and go 2.3 miles to O'Toole Lane. Turn left and follow the dirt road 1.2 miles to its end at Crow Clearing.

Although 3,694-foot Hurricane Mountain is not among the celebrated forty-six High Peaks (it ranks seventy-second in elevation in the Adirondacks), the popular summit boasts a spectacular view and offers birders the possibility of finding a Bicknell's Thrush, a reclusive dweller of subalpine forests. Prior to 1996, this thrush was considered a more southerly subspecies of Gray-cheeked Thrush, but it is now a full species, named for Eugene P. Bicknell, and much sought after by birders (see **Whiteface Highway** for more details). Several males usually maintain territories around the summit of Hurricane, where the Bicknell's can be heard calling or singing and sometimes seen engaging in chase.

The three trails to the top range in distance from 2.6 to 3 miles and in elevation gain from 1,600 to 2,000 feet. Many birders forgo the final uphill pitches, especially in winter.

East Trail (2.7 miles, 1,700-foot ascent): From the gate on Hurricane Mountain Lane, follow the trail uphill through a tunnel of Norway and native spruce, listening for the high notes of Brown Creepers and kinglets and sounds of feeding bands or warbler waves. The trail swings left at the top of the rise, then right into a mixed forest where aspen and birch are reminders of a long-ago forest fire, with conifers now intruding. Passing a hidden small pond and camp on the right, the trail continues upward into a montane boreal belt of balsam fir and spruce. Boreal Chickadee has been found here on almost all of the Elizabethtown Christmas Bird Counts since 1973, with winter finches all along the route, feeding on catkins and cones. In summer, the same stretch is alive with the songs of vireos, thrushes, and warblers. Above the boreal belt is a sudden transition to open beech forest. Some of the old trunks have been clawed by bears. Look also for "bear nests" where the bruins made a seat of branches after stripping them of beechnuts.

The fire tower on Hurricane Mountain

Photo by Phil Brown

Beyond is a stream and lean-to. Next is the final pitch to the summit, but birders are often content to return after reaching the boreal belt. If hiking in winter, bear in mind that the road is plowed only to the last occupied house.

South Trail (2.6 miles, 2,000 feet): The route from Route 9N begins with a short, steep climb through red pine that may have Red Crossbill. A short bushwhack to the right leads over to Pitchoff Mountain (elevation about 2,700 feet). Geoffrey Carleton identified this peak (not the 3,477-foot Pitchoff Mountain eight miles west) as the historic Peregrine Falcon aerie mentioned by John Bull, so the state Department of Environmental Conservation placed one of the first hack sites above this cliff to reintroduce falcons to the Adirondacks in the early 1980s. The trail levels off and becomes an easy walk or ski trip through mixed forest, followed by a stretch of spruce-balsam, where Boreal Chickadee has been found. Beavers have flooded an area near a transition to hardwood and the final ascent. Philadelphia Vireo was found along this trail in early June 2005 and '06. At 2.5 miles, the trail joins the North Trail, marked with red ADK disks. Follow paint blazes on the bare rock to the summit, with its stunning views of the High Peaks and the Champlain Valley, and, with luck, a singing Bicknell's Thrush.

North Trail (3 miles, 1,600 feet): Although this is the longest route, the grades are moderate most of the way. For the first mile or so, from Crow Clearing to the Gulf Brook lean-to, the trail is largely flat. Bear right at the lean-to to climb the mountain. About two miles from Crow Clearing, the trail passes through an attractive forest of white birch, a reminder of fires past. Shortly below the summit, it joins the South Trail. **—JP**

Illustration by Mike Storey

Bicknell's Thrush

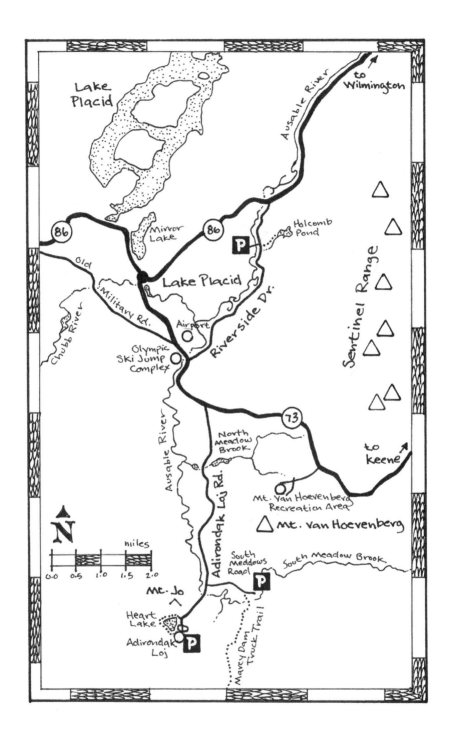

15 Riverside Drive

You may need to tear yourself away from the views of the Sentinel Range and Ausable River to concentrate on the birds. About a hundred species nest in the river corridor, including several of the boreal birds.

DIRECTIONS: From the intersection of NY 86 and NY 73 in Lake Placid, drive south on NY 73 for about 2 miles. Just after passing the Olympic ski jumps and crossing the West Branch of the Ausable River, turn left onto Riverside Drive, also known as River Road. Birding is done along the road and on old trails that lead east into the Sentinel Range Wilderness.

Although birders often have to contend with traffic, four-mile Riverside Drive has long been a popular birding area on the outskirts of Lake Placid. It follows the West Branch of the Ausable River, one of the most celebrated trout streams in the Adirondacks. Of the more than one hundred species of birds that nest near Lake Placid, most can be found along this corridor. Check the fields and open areas along the south end of the road for Savannah Sparrow and other grassland birds, and stop at roadside alder thickets and other brushy areas for Alder Flycatcher, Brown Thrasher, Lincoln's and Swamp Sparrows, and Indigo Bunting. On cloudy days, listen for Wilson's Snipe winnowing overhead. After a while, the road enters more boreal spruce-balsam forest. Watch the tops of tall snags along the Ausable

The Sentinel Range seen from Riverside Drive

for an Olive-sided Flycatcher giving its *pip-pip-pip* call or whistling *quick-three-beers*. Great Blue Heron, Common Merganser, Osprey, and Spotted Sandpiper may flush along the riverside. Stop periodically to walk the road, looking and listening for boreal species: Black-backed Woodpecker, Yellow-bellied Flycatcher, Philadelphia Vireo, Boreal Chickadee, Ruby-crowned Kinglet, and northern finches. Spruce-budworm warblers (Tennessee, Cape May, and Bay-breasted) are always a possibility, and Northern Parula frequent conifers with beard lichen near the water. You may also see Common Raven.

Before the 1932 Winter Olympics, the state built ski trails to South Notch and North Notch on either side of 3,584-foot Slide Mountain. Though no longer maintained, the trails can be followed for a short distance. The old

Photo by Jeff Nadler

Great Blue Heron

South Notch Trail starts on the east side of Riverside Drive about two miles north of Route 73, but most birders continue another mile to a turnoff at the start of the North Notch Trail, where a brook enters the West Branch. Actually, there are two trails here. The one on the left is the North Notch Trail, now washed out by a wetland stream, probably the result of beaver activity. This trail provides a clear view of an Osprey nest that overlooks an open wetland near Holcomb Pond, a good area for flycatchers and Cedar Waxwing. The path continues through conifer forest before ending at a large shrubby wetland, which is rich in warblers, including Nashville, Magnolia, Black-throated Blue, Black-throated Green, and Common Yellowthroat. The other trail, on the right, leads into rich boreal habitat along an old tote road. It soon becomes hard to follow but may provide a Black-backed Woodpecker or other northern species.

Most birders visit the road between spring and fall, but winter can be rewarding. In early winter, the West Branch is one of the few stretches of open water in the Lake Placid area and a good place to find American Black Duck and both Hooded and Common Mergansers. Scan treetops and alders along the south end of the road for Northern Shrike, which shows up regularly. Snow Bunting occurs in the short-grass areas. Boreal Chickadees can be found by spishing and carefully checking responding groups of chickadees and Red-breasted Nuthatches in areas of dense spruce. During invasion years, the river corridor is excellent for winter finches, including White-winged Crossbills —**JP**

Adirondak Loj Road

Pull off to take in one of the iconic Adirondack vistas, then scan the fields for sparrows and swallows. Continue down the road, looking for warblers, flycatchers, Eastern Bluebird, or one of the rarities that turn up from time to time.

DIRECTIONS: From NY 73, about 4 miles southeast of Lake Placid village, turn south onto Adirondak Loj Road, which leads to the lodge operated by the Adirondack Mountain Club (ADK) at Heart Lake. The turn is between the Mt. Van Hoevenberg cross-country ski center and the Olympic ski jumps on the outskirts of Lake Placid. Follow the road 3.5 miles south to South Meadow Road on the left, a mile-long dirt road providing a side trip to South Meadow and Marcy Dam Truck Trail. Return to the main road and continue another 1.2 miles to the Adirondak Loj parking lot and Heart Lake, where the road ends. See map, p. 70.

In April 1903, a farmer lost control of a grass fire that smoldered in the duff until springing to life as a crown fire in early June, burning eight miles in less than three hours and destroying the Adirondack Lodge (the phonetic spelling had yet to be adopted), which had opened in 1880, and most of the woods along Heart Lake Road, as it was formerly called. Ornithologist Aretas Saunders spent July and August of 1925 and '26 at the old Wood Farm at the north end of the road, and the noted observer Geoffrey Carleton birded here from July 1932 into the 1980s. Saunders found the area "now covered with a growth of aspen and fire cherry. Here and there young maples, spruces, and balsams are coming in, and the locality is no longer unsightly, but indeed attractive." Saunders found a singing

Algonquin Peak dominates the horizon from Adirondak Loj Road.

Photo by Susan Bibeau

Philadelphia Vireo near Alcohol Brook (now North Meadow Brook) near the Wood Farm in 1926, the first summer record for the state, and Carleton again found singing males here in 1932-33, "in second growth about 20 or 25 feet high, mainly maple, poplar and cherry, mixed with open brambly patches–land once burnt over." Today much of the same area is now bordered by maturing mixed forest and conifers, including naturalized Norway spruce along Adirondak Loj Road and stands of Scotch pine bordering South Meadow Road, both apparently planted sometime in the wake of the 1903 fire, perhaps by the Civilian Conservation Corps during the Depression. Despite habitat changes, the road still offers superb birding.

At the start of the road, watch the large open field on the right for Vesper and Savannah Sparrows and the wires overhead for Ruby-throated Hummingbird and swallows. At the first curve to the right, the old trail leading down to an abandoned dam at North Meadow is now brushed in, and a large house now occupies the field beyond that led to a boreal pocket where the first nest of Wilson's Warbler in New York State was found in July 1978, Cape May Warbler nested in the 1980s, and a Sedge Wren was banded in 1994. A Northern Hawk Owl spent the winter of November 1992-April 1993 in this same area, sometimes with Bohemian Waxwing. Also, a singing Clay-colored Sparrow was here in June 2000. Stop at the bridge over North Meadow Brook and listen for warblers and other birds. A Ruddy Turnstone along the brook in September 1976 was a surprise, but Eastern Bluebirds are more likely to be found here, around the nearby farmhouse.

Continue through forest to South Meadow Road, turn left, and drive to the end (in winter, the road is not plowed). From the parking lot, walk a few hundred yards on the Klondike Notch Trail to South Meadow Brook, one of the headwaters of the West Branch of the Ausable River, and listen for Olive-sided and Alder Flycatchers. After returning to the lot, follow a path that leads southwest from the lot to the **Marcy Dam** Truck Trail (which is closed to vehicles). Just past the trail register a bridge crosses South Meadow Brook. A Lark Sparrow was found among Chipping Sparrows in this area in September 1981, and Eastern Phoebes may have a nest under the bridge.

Return to Adirondak Loj Road and continue to the ADK parking lot, where a fee is charged. Walk west to the Adirondak Loj on the shores of Heart Lake, the start of trails that circle the lake and go up nearby Mount Jo, where Blackpoll Warbler nest near the 2,876-foot summit. Saunders advised, "The traveler will do well to walk the Heart Lake Road, at least once," but today most choose to drive. **—JP**

17 Marcy Dam

Take an easy hike to a mountain pond while listening to the music of wood warblers. Least Flycatcher and Swainson's Thrush can be found at the pond. If you continue to Lake Colden, you could see a Bicknell's Thrush or one of the boreal birds.

DIRECTIONS: Take the Adirondak Loj Road 4.8 miles south to the parking lot and hikers building near Adirondak Loj. (The Adirondack Mountain Club charges a fee for parking.) Follow the Van Hoevenburg Trail with blue markers 2.4 miles south to Marcy Dam. (The 2.8-mile truck trail from South Meadow Road offers an alternate route to Marcy Dam. See directions for **Adirondak Loj**.) Just past the dam, the Van Hoevenburg Trail bears left to go to Indian Falls and Mount Marcy. The trail right, marked by yellow disks, leads to Avalanche Pass and Lake Colden.

Before setting off on the trail, take a walk over to the nearby Loj on the shores of Heart Lake and enjoy the summer songs of Winter Wrens, Ruby-crowned Kinglets, Rose-breasted Grosbeaks, Purple Finches, and a host of other forest birds. The conifers and shrubs around the Loj contain a wider variety of species than found along the trail. An American Three-toed Woodpecker was found here in April 1998.

The hike to Marcy Dam (elevation 2,365 feet) entails a gradual climb of just 187 feet in 2.4 miles. Most of the trail is through hardwoods. A quarter-mile from the register, the trail crosses MacIntyre Brook; the wet thickets are a good spot for Canada Warbler. Other warblers commonly heard singing

A rare sighting: paddlers at Marcy Dam

along the trail include Black-throated Blue, Black-throated Green, and Blackburnian. After nearly two miles, Marcy Brook can be heard and then seen on the left. Philadelphia Vireo nests were found here in June 1975 and at Marcy Dam in June of 1963. This vireo of medium-elevation second-growth hardwoods was found on the Avalanche Pass Trail about a mile above the dam, at about 2,600 feet, near Avalanche Camps in June 2003. Most singing vireos will be Red-eyed, however, or perhaps Blue-headed in areas with conifers, and most birds of all species will be heard singing in the canopy, rather than seen, until the dam.

Marcy Dam (the name applies to the small lake, as well as the dam itself) stands at the site of an old lumber dam used for driving logs down Marcy Brook. Today the shoreline of the lake is a popular camping place, with tent sites and lean-tos. The local Black-capped Chickadees are known to be the boldest in the Adirondacks and quite adept at stealing a bit of lunch. Least Flycatcher, Ovenbird, and Swainson's Thrush can be heard singing from the woods, while Tree Swallows skim over the water. The round trip from Adirondak Loj or South Meadow Road is a pleasant hike or cross-country ski trip that offers an opportunity to hear and see a variety of species away from the noise of traffic.

For the more adventuresome, Marcy Dam marks the starting point of trips into the High Peaks and the possibility of more boreal birdlife. At 4.4 miles from the Loj, the Van Hoevenberg Trail passes Indian Falls, where American Three-toed Woodpecker was found in July 1980. As the trail nears tree line on the way to Little Marcy, Swainson's Thrush begins to give way to the rarer Bicknell's Thrush. The trail to Avalanche Pass has Yellow-bellied Flycatchers in summer and White-winged Crossbills during invasion winters. Avalanche Lake, on the other side of the pass, had Cape May Warbler in June 1981. Farther on, Lake Colden and the Flowed Lands provide possibilities of both Black-backed and American Three-toed Woodpeckers, Boreal Chickadee, Bicknell's Thrush, and Bay-breasted and Blackpoll Warblers. **—JP**

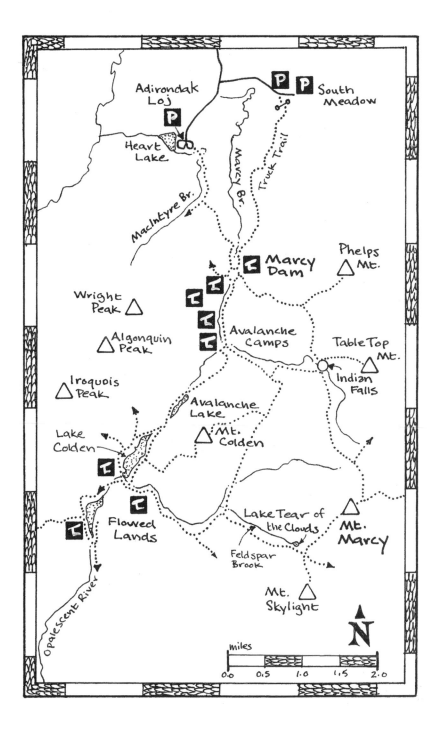

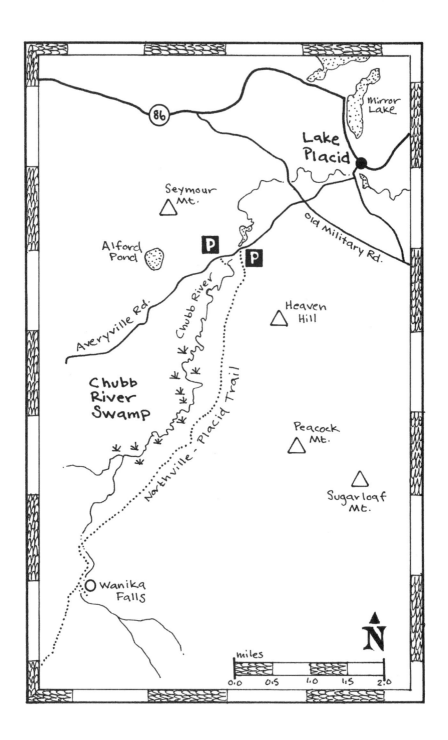

Chubb River Swamp

Paddle up a quiet stream to a vast marsh in the heart of the High Peaks Wilderness, looking and listening for Northern Parula, Black-backed Woodpecker, and Rusty Blackbird, among other species.

DIRECTIONS: From the junction of NY 73 and NY 86 in Lake Placid, head south on NY 73 for 0.2 miles to Averyville Road. Turn right and go 2.2 miles, crossing Old Military Road, to a parking area on the left, just before a bridge over the Chubb River. If paddling, drive over the bridge and look for an unmarked portage trail on the left, near the top a small hill.

Chubb River Swamp has long been a favored birding area, but in recent decades the old trail along the eastern bank has become brushed in. Access was always difficult due to quicksand-like mudholes and blowdown, but the trail is now but a memory in places, and so most birders opt for travel on the river itself by canoe, kayak, cross-country skis, or snowshoes. John Bull (1974) included a color plate of a lovely painting of this boreal forest by Al Gilbert, showing the spruce-balsam association occupied by Spruce Grouse, Black-backed Woodpecker, Gray Jay, Boreal Chickadee, Ruby-crowned Kinglet, Bay-breasted Warbler, and Evening Grosbeak, observing, "All of the above breed in or near this locality."

Paddlers take in the scenery on the Chubb River.

A short distance from the parking area, the Northville-Placid Trail now branches off to the left, climbing a ridge above the river. Although the hiking is easier and drier than on the old trail, the higher route quickly changes to mixed and largely deciduous forest with far fewer opportunities for boreal birds. Birders generally ignore this turnoff and continue a few hundred feet or so to the river and a large rock. The old trail curves to the left here and may still be traced along the east bank of the Chubb River by those willing to bushwhack large stretches. The rock also had been the starting point for paddling or ski trips on the river before the state built a short portage trail from Averyville Road to a put-in on the opposite bank.

Birding on the Chubb carries several caveats, the most important being that travel in winter on river ice requires extended cold and solid ice. One of the highlights but also one of the drawbacks of travel on the river is a series of upstream beaver dams that must be crossed. Paddlers will have to haul their canoes or kayaks over them. In winter, even when the ice is quite solid, it can be soft in the vicinity of the dams, so passage should be near the shoreline and caution observed. The river provides wide vistas of the bordering forest and excellent viewing of many birds in a pristine setting free of vehicles.

Birdsong carries well over the river. Northern Parula may sing from lichen-draped spruces in summer and White-winged Crossbills from atop the same trees in winters with a bumper cone crop. Each band of Black-capped Chickadees usually has a few Boreal Chickadees and Golden-crowned Kinglets, and the most common woodpecker may be the Black-backed Woodpecker, often found drumming or feeding on standing dead snags. Spruce Grouse was last reported in the 1980s, and Gray Jay is extremely rare, if still present, but the variety of other boreal species is good. In summer listen for the "creaky-door" call of Rusty Blackbird, and in winter look for their three-tiered used nests in speckled alders along the bank.

The river eventually reaches a short stretch of rapids with a portage trail on the left, providing easy passage around the rapids for canoeists or skiers, or a spot to have lunch and turn around. Above the rapids, the river winds through a vast marsh with impressive views of mountains in the High Peaks Wilderness. However far they choose to go, visitors will appreciate why both John Bull and Geoffrey Carleton recommended Chubb River Swamp. **—JP**

⑲ Whiteface Highway

Drive to the top of the fifth-highest mountain in the state, soak in the views, and bird the highway on the way down. There's no easier way to find the reclusive Bicknell's Thrush, a coveted species that breeds only at high elevations.

DIRECTIONS: From NY 86 in Wilmington, take NY 431 northwest, passing the North Pole and Santa's Workshop, to the Veterans Memorial Highway tollbooth. Take the highway 5.3 miles uphill to the Castle, which houses a restaurant, and a spectacular lookout just below the 4,867-foot summit of Whiteface. A walkway leads 0.2 miles to the actual summit. Birding is best delayed until the return drive.

The Whiteface Mountain Veterans Memorial Highway rises almost 3,850 feet from the hamlet of Wilmington to the parking area just below the summit and offers the opportunity to see a variety of Adirondack birds. Birding traffic has seen an increase nearly as steep as the road itself during the past decade. This is the only highway in the Adirondack Park that rises into the high-elevation breeding range of Bicknell's Thrush, a boreal bird that nests in upstate New York (Adirondacks and Catskills), New England, and portions of Québec and the Maritimes. Blackpoll Warbler is also frequent near the summit.

The weather station on Whiteface Mountain

Photo by Susan Bibeau

Early visitors climbed Whiteface Mountain, fifth highest of the forty-six High Peaks, by foot or horseback, following trails from Franklin Falls, Lake Placid, and Wilmington. Some ascended by the bedrock slide that gives the mountain its name. In 1921, New York State acquired Whiteface and 4,500 acres of spruce forest, which became part of the forever-wild Forest Preserve. Over the objections of conservationists, the state built a road to the top as a tribute to World War I veterans, finishing in 1935.

Bicknell's Thrush, the species sought by most Whiteface birders, was not recognized as a full species until 1995. The bird was named for Eugene P. Bicknell, who discovered a new breeding thrush on Slide Mountain in the Catskills in 1881. The next year Robert Ridgeway described *bicknelli* as a smaller subspecies of the more widespread Gray-cheeked Thrush of northern Canada, Alaska, and northeastern Siberia, which had been recognized as a species since 1858. Following this news, C. Hart Merriam ruefully reported, "In my cabinet is a specimen of this recently described Thrush which I shot in Lewis County, near the western border of the Adirondacks, May 24, 1878," or over three years before Bicknell's discovery. If not for this lapse, birders might be seeking Merriam's Thrush. The nesting range of this thrush was mapped and its history outlined in *The Atlas of Breeding Birds in New York State*. By 1992, the first Adirondack survey of what was still called "Bicknell's" Gray-cheeked Thrush had begun. Then in 1993, Henri Ouellet of Québec proposed that Bicknell's and Gray-cheeked Thrushes are distinct species, based upon his studies of measurements, plumage, soft-part colors, and songs. A seminal article by Ian McLaren of Nova Scotia appeared in *Birding* in 1995, and soon after the American Ornithologists' Union pronounced Bicknell's Thrush to be a valid species. The rush to see this bird was on, with Whiteface one of the most popular destinations.

Bicknell's is most easily seen at and between the two hairpin turns (Lake Placid and Wilmington) near the summit. Also check the road below the Lake Placid turn to the next bend. Listen for its song especially in the morning shortly after the toll road opens to vehicles. Early June and September are best. Do not use recordings to lure this globally uncommon species.

Before driving to the mountain, check www.whiteface.com for dates and times that the tollbooth is open. If it's closed, you may walk up the road without charge or take one of two hiking trails. The view of the High Peaks and Lake Placid is well worth the trip even if you don't encounter a Bicknell's. **—JP**

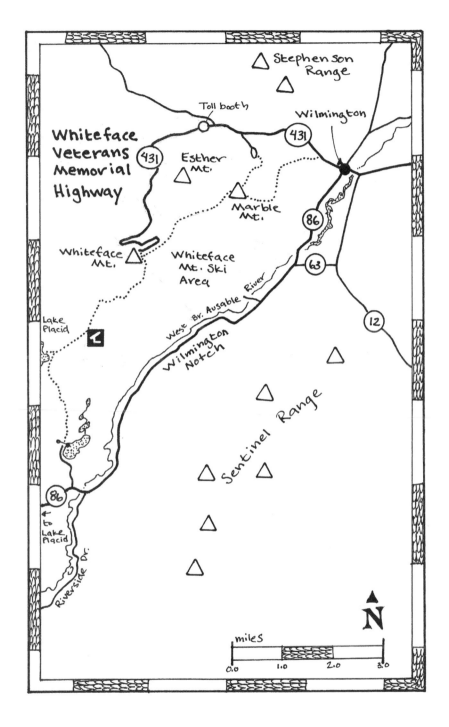

Stephenson Range

Toll booth

Wilmington

431

Whiteface Veterans Memorial Highway

431

Esther Mt.

Marble Mt.

86

Whiteface Mt.

Whiteface Mt. Ski Area

63

West Br. Ausable River

Lake Placid

12

Wilmington Notch

Sentinel Range

86

← to Lake Placid

Riverside Dr.

N

miles

0.0   1.0   2.0   3.0

Photo by Kurt K. Burnham

Peregrine Falcon chicks

Finding Peregrines

Peregrine Falcons have come back strong since the days of DDT. In the mid-1960s, there were no peregrines east of the Mississippi. After the pesticide was banned in 1972, DEC began a "hacking" program in the Adirondacks. Chicks hatched in captivity were placed on cliffs and fed by humans until they could fend for themselves. Falcons started nesting in the state again in 1983, on bridges in New York City. Today, they nest on numerous bridges (and a few cliffs) in the Hudson Valley and on skyscrapers in several cities. In the Adirondacks, you can observe falcons in a more natural setting.

Peregrines build nests on a number of high ledges in the northern Adirondacks and Lake George region. The falcons usually arrive in April. Each spring, DEC enlists the aid of rock climbers and birders to determine the locations of active nests, and the agency closes climbing routes that will disturb the falcons. In 2007, at least twelve pairs raised chicks.

Birders can call DEC at 518-897-1291 or check the agency's Web site to find out where the nests are. The best places to observe the falcons are the cliffs in the Chapel Pond region along Route 73 in Keene Valley, on Poke-O-Moonshine Mountain, whose wide rock face is conspicuous from Route 9 just south of Northway Exit 33, and at Wilmington Notch on Route 86 east of Lake Placid.

Peregrine acrobatics are fascinating to watch. Diving to attack prey in midair, they can exceed two hundred miles an hour. Females typically lay two to four eggs, which hatch in middle or late May. The chicks fledge in six weeks and soon begin soaring, swooping, and dogfighting with their siblings. They kill their first prey after eight or nine weeks. Parents and offspring usually leave the nest in late July or early August. Adults may overwinter in the vicinity of their aeries, especially along Lake Champlain.

Silver Lake Bog

Follow the boardwalk through a bog that shelters several of the boreal birds. Continue hiking to a bluff overlooking Silver Lake to see wood warblers, hawks, and perhaps a Bald Eagle.

DIRECTIONS: From NY 86 in Wilmington, turn onto Bonnieview Road and follow it the end (about 6 miles), where it meets County 17. Turn left and go roughly 6.5 miles to Union Falls Road, reached just after passing Silver Lake. Bear left and go 1.5 miles to Old Hawkeye Road (dirt) on the left. Turn and go about a half-mile down the road to a parking area on the right.

The Adirondack Nature Conservancy owns a sixty-one-acre preserve that encompasses the bog and some bluffs overlooking Silver Lake. Despite its small size, the preserve contains a variety of habitats: a black spruce-tamarack bog, Northern white cedar swamp, a hemlock-Northern hardwood forest, a pine ridge (the bluffs), and a piece of the Silver Lake shoreline. Pamphlets at the trailhead describe the flora and fauna.

A handicapped-accessible boardwalk leads you across the bog, about a half-mile. Then a footpath climbs two hundred feet to the bluffs, with views of the lake and Whiteface Mountain. The round trip is about two and a half miles.

Bluffs overlooking Silver Lake

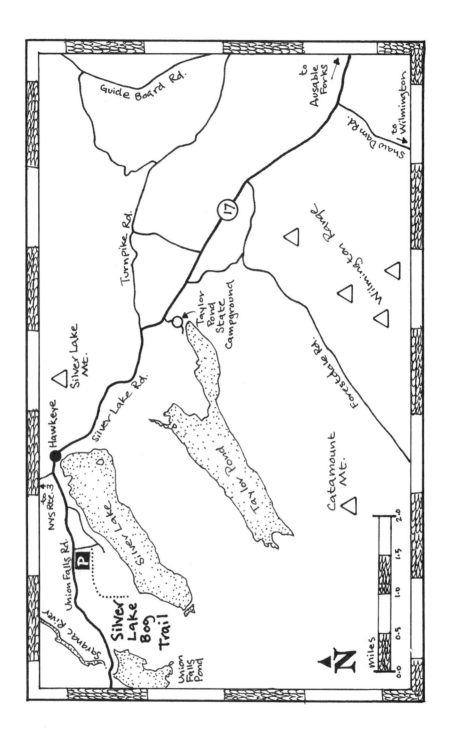

In that half-mile on the boardwalk you can find most of the boreal birds, including Black-backed Woodpecker, which often nests within sight of the trail. Other species seen and heard from the boardwalk are Boreal and Black-capped Chickadees, Golden-crowned and Ruby-crowned Kinglets, Northern Parula, Nashville Warbler, Red-breasted Nuthatch, Purple Finch, and Olive-sided and Yellow-bellied Flycatchers.

There are lots of interesting plants in the bog, such as creeping snowberry, sheep laurel, Labrador tea, pitcher plant, bog cranberry, twinflower, and several kinds of sedges, all growing on a mat of sphagnum moss. The creeping snowberry is a small round-leaf vine that spreads over the moss. In July, it produces a small white berry with a strong mint taste. I call it nature's Tic-Tac. It takes only a couple to reflavor your stale gum.

After the boardwalk, the trail ascends through a hardwood forest to the red pines on the bluff. Look for pink lady's slippers under the pines. Most of the other wood warblers can be found on the hike to the bluff, plus Scarlet Tanager, Rose-breasted Grosbeak, Least Flycatcher, and Pileated and Hairy Woodpeckers. Stay awhile at the lookout as you may see a soaring Bald Eagle, Red-tailed Hawk, or Broad-winged Hawk. **—GL**

Least Flycatcher

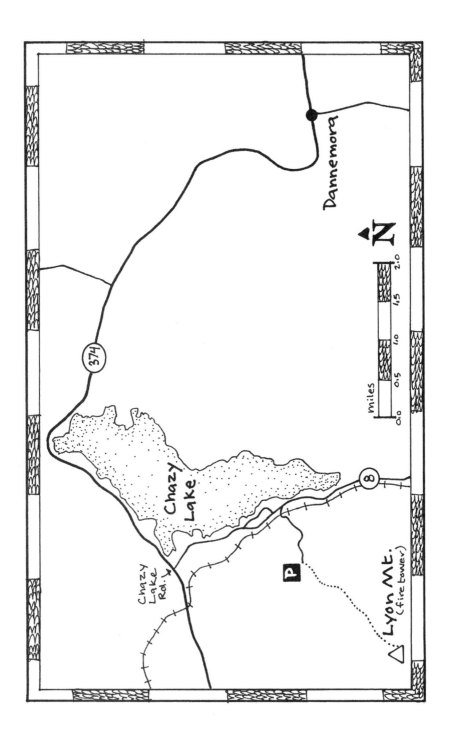

㉑ Lyon Mountain

Enjoy the panoramic view from a restored fire tower after climbing through a changing forest and observing a variety of woodland birds. On the summit, you may see Bicknell's Thrush or Common Raven.

DIRECTIONS: From the village of Dannemora, drive west on NY 374 for 9.3 miles to Chazy Lake Road and turn left. Go 1.7 miles to a dirt road on the right. Go up the dirt road for almost a mile to a parking area. The trail begins on the south side of the lot.

Lyon Mountain is the northernmost peak in the state where birders can find Bicknell's Thrush, which nests only at high elevations. At 3,820 feet, Lyon Mountain nearly qualifies as an Adirondack High Peak. From the parking area, the trail climbs more than 1,900 feet to a refurbished fire tower. On a clear day, you can see all the way to Montreal. The view also takes in northern Lake Champlain, the Green Mountains of Vermont, and many of the High Peaks.

The original trail went pretty much straight up the mountain for 2.5 miles. It was rough and often full of cobble. In 2008, the Adirondack Mountain Club built a new trail with plenty of switchbacks. It's not as steep, but it's about a mile longer.

Starting at the parking area, you can hear Black-throated Green, Black-throated Blue, and Blackburnian Warblers, Veery, Ovenbird, American

Photo by Mike Lynch

The refurbished fire tower on Lyon Mountain

Redstart, Scarlet Tanager, Winter Wren, White-throated Sparrow, Ruffed Grouse, Northern Flicker, and Red-eyed, Yellow-throated, and Blue-headed Vireos. As you go higher, you should continue to hear the warblers as well as Hermit Thrush. After a few miles, start listening for Swainson's Thrush.

On one trip, I heard at the higher elevations Yellow-bellied Flycatcher, Golden-crowned Kinglet, Boreal Chickadee, Blackpoll Warbler, and, closer to the top, Bicknell's Thrush. I also saw a Bicknell's on the summit while I was picking blueberries; I think I was in its berry patch. Also up on top were Dark-eyed Junco, White-throated Sparrow, Yellow-rumped Warbler, and a pair of ravens riding updrafts from the lake. I watched five Turkey Vultures soaring in the valley east of the mountain for a half-hour; sometimes they came so close I felt that I could reach out and touch them.

You don't have to climb the mountain to find good birds. Judy Heintz, who has birded the area for years, says you can come across a variety of species along the entrance road and the power-line corridor that crosses it. Among them are Northern Waterthrush; Alder, Willow, Least, and Great Crested Flycatchers; Philadelphia, Blue-headed, and Red-eyed Vireos; Tennessee, Black-and-white, Golden-winged, Chestnut-sided, Mourning, and Magnolia Warblers, and occasionally Canada Warblers. You may also spot such interesting birds as Cliff Swallow, Baltimore Oriole, and Brown Thrasher along the power line and adjacent hedgerows.

Photo by J.M.C. Peterson

Magnolia Warbler

If you have a canoe or kayak, go for a paddle on Chazy Lake. South of the Lyon Mountain access road, you can find informal put-ins along Chazy Lake Road. Paddle to the marshy area near the inlet at the south end of the lake. A Bald Eagle has been hanging out there in recent years. Watch for Hooded and Common Mergansers, Mallards, and Wood, American Black, and Ring-necked Ducks and listen for the calls of American Bittern and Virginia Rail. Two pairs of Common Loon nest on the lake. You may also find Marsh Wren. Keep an eye on the sky for Peregrine Falcons, which nest near Upper Chateaugay Lake on the other side of the mountain. **—GL**

Northern Region
Birding in the Boreal Belt

22. Whitney Wilderness
23. Bog River & Lows Lake
24. Five Ponds Wilderness
25. Peavine Swamp
26. Massawepie Mire
27. Tupper Lake Marsh
28. Floodwood Road
29. Spring Pond Bog
30. St. Regis Canoe Area
31. Paul Smiths VIC
32. Madawaska
33. Jones & Osgood Ponds
34. Bloomingdale Bog
35. Bigelow Road
36. Saranac Lake Village
37. California Road
    & Debar Pond

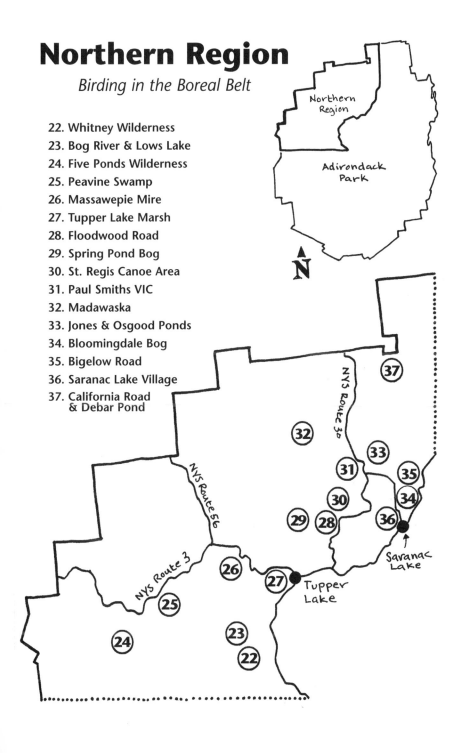

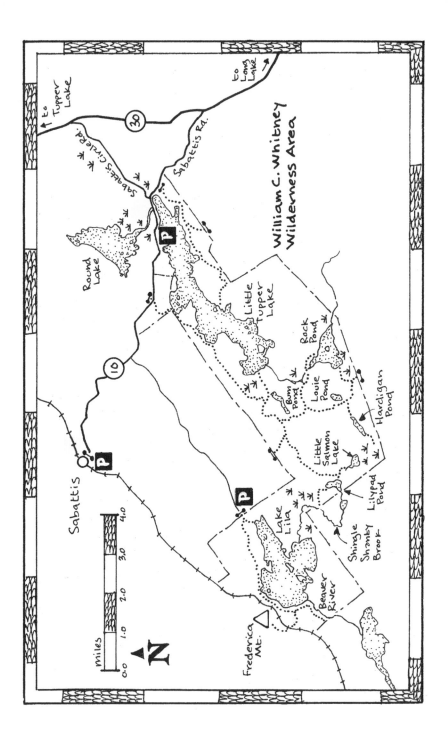

㉒ Whitney Wilderness

Bring a canoe or kayak to explore wilderness lakes where Gray Jay, Boreal Chickadee, Black-backed Woodpecker, Osprey, and a variety of wood warblers can be found. The rare Spruce Grouse also has been sighted here.

DIRECTIONS: From the junction of NY 28N and NY 30 in Long Lake, drive north on NY 30 for 6 miles to Sabattis Road. Turn left and go 2.5 miles to an intersection with Sabattis Circle Road. Bear left, continuing on Sabattis Road, and drive 1 mile to the parking lot on the left for Little Tupper Lake. To reach Lake Lila, keep going on Sabattis Road for another 2 miles and turn left onto a dirt road (which usually opens about Memorial Day). There is a parking lot at the end of this 5-mile road. A 0.3-mile trail leads from the lot to Lake Lila. If you are coming from Tupper Lake, turn right off NY 30 onto Sabattis Circle Road, which is reached 9.6 miles after crossing the Raquette River.

Little Tupper Lake and Lake Lila are the biggest waterbodies in the William C. Whitney Wilderness. Both are non-motorized lakes with primitive campsites. On windy days, they can get rough in a short time, so paddlers need to be cautious.

From Little Tupper, you can canoe up the inlet to Rock Pond or down the outlet to Round Lake. On the big lake, you may find Common Loons nesting or with young. Merlins have nested next to the parking lot. Bald Eagles are often seen. The shoreline is a mix of softwood and hardwood trees, so you can hear most of the wood warblers singing somewhere around the lake. Boreal habitat isn't that far away, so there's always the pos-

Lake Lila

sibility of seeing northern birds, especially if you paddle to Round Lake or Rock Pond. Round Lake also has two pairs of nesting loons.

In recent years, Lake Lila has had a pair of nesting Osprey on the shoreline as well as nesting loons on the lake. Wood warblers sing in the forest along the water. Boreal birds inhabit much of the area. A Cape May Warbler was seen once right in the parking lot. If you canoe to the west end of the lake, where Nehasane Lodge once stood, you'll find boreal habitat that supports Gray Jay, Boreal Chickadee, and Black-backed Woodpecker. You also can find wood warblers in the vicinity. Another option is to hike about three miles to the site of the old lodge, following a dirt lane (closed to vehicles) from the parking lot. The rare and elusive Spruce Grouse has

Photo by Jeff Nadler

Red Crossbill

been seen in recent years on the south side of the lake. Just before the lodge site, you'll pass another dirt road on the right. This leads to a short trail that climbs Mount Frederica, whose ledges offer a nice view of the lake.

While you're in the neighborhood, check out the beautiful bog on Sabattis Circle Road. It's on the north side of the road. Many interesting boreal species can be found here, including Gray Jay and Boreal Chickadee in the taller spruce and fir trees. Palm Warbler and Lincoln's

Sparrow are heard singing in early summer. When there is a good cone crop, look for both White-winged and Red Crossbills in winter.

You can visit another bog by driving up Sabattis Road past the Lake Lila access road to the railroad tracks at the old Sabattis Station. Hike the tracks to the northeast a very short distance to find many of most-sought-after birds, such as Northern Saw-whet and Short-eared Owls and Northern Parula. It's good winter birding, too, but bring snowshoes. You might see White-winged and Red Crossbills, Pine Siskins, and Common Redpolls during good cone years. **—GL**

23 Bog River & Lows Lake

Paddle up the Bog River to Hitchins Pond on a day trip or go farther and camp out on Lows Lake. Either way, you'll pass through excellent boreal habitat. Lows Lake boasts one of the Park's largest populations of Common Loon.

DIRECTIONS: Just south of Tupper Lake (the lake, not the community) on NY 30, turn west onto County 421, which goes past Bog River Falls to Horseshoe Lake. After 5.8 miles, just after the pavement ends, turn left onto a dirt road that leads in 0.75 miles to the Lower Dam on the Bog River. The turn is marked by a wooden sign. DEC publishes a free leaflet titled "Bog River Flow Map and Guide."

The three-mile flatwater paddle up the Bog River from the Lower Dam to Hitchins Pond, which can easily be done in a day, takes you through excellent habitat for boreal birds. Look and listen for, among others, Boreal Chickadee and Gray Jay. Many wood warblers and thrushes also can be found. Just after passing under a railroad bridge, you'll enter a boggy area where Short-eared Owl nested in 2005. A pair of Common Loons lives on Hitchins Pond, and Bald Eagles are often seen hunting there. Many different ducks are found along the pond, which is really a weedy stretch of the river.

From the southwest end of the pond, there is a short carry to the Upper Dam at the foot of Lows Lake. If you really want to explore this nine-mile lake (originally part of the Bog River), plan on spending the night at one of the forty shoreline campsites. The Hiawatha Boy Scouts Council has exclusive

Photo by Phil Brown

View of Hitchins Pond and the Bog River from Lows Ridge

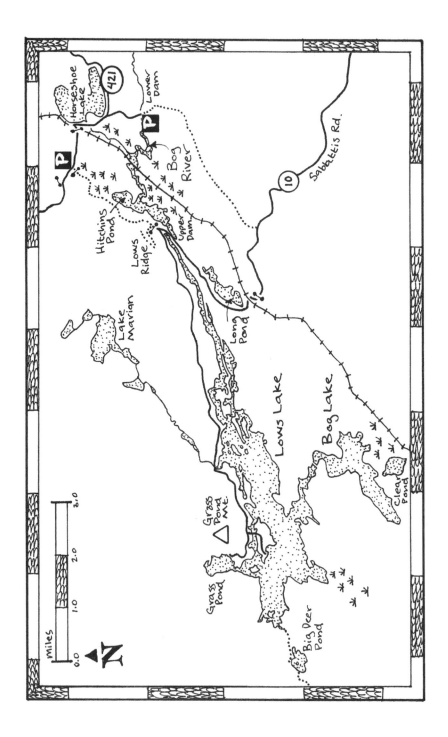

rights to some islands and campsites, as indicated in DEC's leaflet. The lake boasts eight pairs of nesting loons–the second-largest concentration in the state. Many of the birds have been banded and are monitored by the Adirondack Loon Conservation Program. A pair of Bald Eagles has nested on the lake since 2001. Great Blue Herons often feed along the water's edge.

Lows Lake has a large floating bog mat, which is a good place to look for migrating shorebirds in late summer. When I was banding loons near the mat one night in the summer of 2007, I was serenaded by a chorus of frogs, Barred Owls, and loons. With all the moths we saw that night, I'm sure Northern Saw-whet Owls were having a feast.

Both conifers and hardwoods grow along the shore of Lows Lake, providing many species in the region places to nest, including the boreal birds, wood warblers, thrushes, flycatchers, and Scarlet Tanager.

At the west end of Lows Lake, there is a 3.5-mile canoe carry that goes past Big Deer Pond to the Oswegatchie River. It's a sixteen-mile paddle downriver to Inlet, with one short carry around High Falls. There are many beaver dams to go over above High Falls. This area was hit by the 1995 windstorm, so it's a changing evergreen forest, with good boreal-bird habitat. A car shuttle is needed for this trip. See **Five Ponds Wilderness** for more information about the birds you can expect to see. **—GL**

Hike to Hitchins

Some birders prefer walking to Hitchins Pond via an old dirt road (closed to vehicles) that passes a large peatland, a wetland marsh, and forests with both coniferous and hardwood trees. Birds that may be seen during the two-and-a-half-mile walk include Black-backed Woodpecker, Gray Jay, Palm Warbler, Magnolia Warbler, Canada Warbler, Northern Waterthrush, Lincoln's Sparrow, Red-shouldered and Broad-winged Hawks, Evening Grosbeak, Common Raven, and Bald Eagle. At the end of the trail, turn left for the pond or right to hike the one-mile trail up Lows Ridge for views of the Bog River. **Directions:** *Continue on Route 421 past the turn for the Lower Dam. The trail is on the left 0.9 miles past the railroad tracks.*

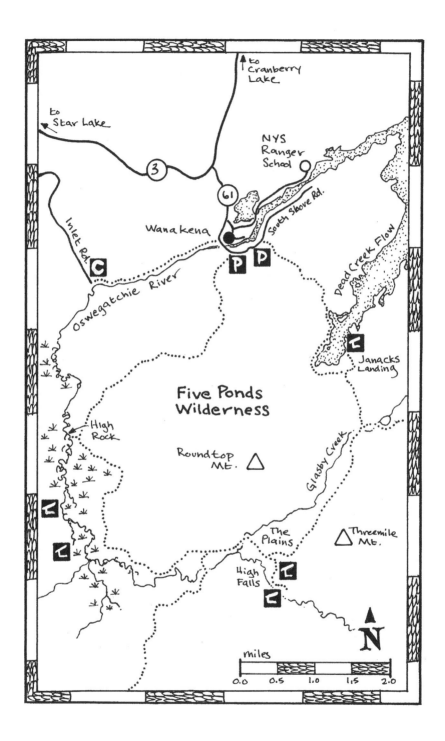

to Cranberry Lake

to Star Lake

3

61

NYS Ranger School

South Shore Rd.

Wanakena

Inlet Rd.

C

P P

Oswegatchie River

Dead Creek Flow

Janacks Landing

Five Ponds Wilderness

High Rock

Roundtop Mt. △

Glasby Creek

The Plains

△ Threemile Mt.

High Falls

N

miles

0.0   0.5   1.0   1.5   2.0

Five Ponds Wilderness

Whether you hike the High Falls Loop or paddle up the Oswegatchie River, you're sure to see some wild country and interesting birds, such as Ruby-crowned Kinglet, Northern Parula, Winter Wren, and perhaps American Three-toed Woodpecker.

DIRECTIONS: The High Falls loop starts in Wanakena. From Cranberry Lake, drive west on NY 3, passing over the Oswegatchie River. At 6.7 miles beyond the river, turn left onto County 61. Bear right at two intersections. About 1.5 miles from NY 3, just after crossing the Oswegatchie again, look for a gravel road on the right. This is the western leg of the loop, which passes High Rock. Keep driving to a parking area on the right past the tennis court. The trailhead for the eastern leg is about a half-mile farther up the road. Those paddling up the Oswegatchie should continue on NY 3 for 2.9 miles beyond the Wanakena turn to Sunny Lake (or Inlet) Road. Turn here and drive 3 miles to the put-in.

There are many ways to venture into the Five Ponds Wilderness, a 118,000-acre tract in the northwestern Adirondacks between **Stillwater Reservoir** and Cranberry Lake. From the south, you can paddle across the reservoir to pick up the Red Horse Trail, starting at the Trout Pond lean-to, and hike north past Salmon Lake and Witchhopple Lake to Clear Pond, a distance of 5.3 miles. From the east, you can canoe to the head of **Lows Lake**, portage to Big Deer Pond and the Oswegatchie River, and then paddle downstream sixteen miles to the take-out at Inlet. For an easier trip, canoeists can start at Inlet (a put-in west of Wanakena) and paddle upriver and back. From the west, you can hike to Hog Pond and Tied Lake (1.0 mile) or to Upper South Pond (1.8 miles). But perhaps the simplest way to see the Five Ponds Wilderness is to hike all or part of the eighteen-mile High Falls Loop. Given the distance, many birders will want to camp out at the falls or along the trail or turn around short of the falls.

A hiker on the High Falls Loop

Photo by Phil Brown

Photo by Carl Heilman II

High Rock overlooking the Oswegatchie River

Whatever you choose to do, if you spend enough time in this region you're bound to see or hear just about every bird in the North Country. Tom Salo, who explored the area around the reservoir for the second edition of the state breeding-bird atlas, said the only boreal birds he missed in his travels were Palm Warbler and Rusty Blackbird—and that may have been because he didn't get into any big bogs. He scored with most of the warblers, though Northern Parula was heard infrequently. He also saw Merlin, Bald Eagle, and Red-tailed, Broad-winged, Cooper's, and Sharp-shinned Hawks. Altogether, more than seventy species have been found in the area.

On my trips into the Five Ponds Wilderness, I have heard many Northern Waterthrushes. Common Loons can be found on most of the bigger lakes in the region. One recent fall, I hiked to Witchhopple Lake and found a pair of loons still feeding a big chick. Various ducks, including Wood, Ring-necked, and American Black, and both Common and Hooded Mergansers can be found on the lakes and ponds.

The High Falls Loop begins and ends in Wanakena, a tiny hamlet on the Oswegatchie that is home to the New York State Ranger School. There are two trailheads on South Shore Road. Start at the western trailhead, near some tennis courts, and hike south along Skate Creek toward High Rock, which overlooks the Oswegatchie as it snakes through an alder swamp. The short spur trail to High Rock is reached at 3.7 miles. Don't miss the view! For those who don't want to hike the whole loop, High Rock or the beaver meadow farther south is a good turnaround spot. As it continues south, the main trail, marked by red disks, eventually pulls alongside the river. At 8.0 miles, it reaches a junction with the trail to the Five Ponds (which passes through the largest stand of virgin forest in the Northeast), and at 8.8 miles, it comes to a spur trail that leads 0.4 miles to High Falls, where the river drops twenty feet. The falls are 9.2 miles from South Shore Road. There are two lean-tos, one on either side of the river, but they are often occupied in summer.

The hike is flat the whole way to the falls. The trail passes through a variety of woods, wetlands, and river habitat. Some of the boreal species you may encounter are Black-backed and American Three-toed Woodpeckers, Gray Jay, and Boreal Chickadee. Many warblers have been found along the trail, including Blackburnian, Black-throated Blue, Black-throated Green, Nashville, Canada, Mourning, Northern Parula, and Yellow-rumped. Golden-crowned and Ruby-crowned Kinglets also nest in the area, and Winter Wrens often can be heard singing along the trail.

Once back on the main trail, you can turn left to retrace your route or turn right to return to South Shore Road on a trail marked at first by blue disks, later by red disks. This trail skirts the Plains, a large tract of grass and brush, and climbs to a saddle between Roundtop and Threemile mountains. After crossing Glasby Creek, it descends to Dead Creek Flow, an arm of Cranberry Lake, and follows an old railroad bed to the eastern trailhead, a distance of 8.7 miles from the falls. From the trailhead, you'll need to walk on South Shore Road for a half-mile to get back to your car.

An equally delightful way to get to High Falls is by canoe. From Inlet, it's thirteen miles upriver to the falls. On the way, you'll pass lean-tos at Griffin Rapids and the Cage Lake Springhole. The other option is the Oswegatchie Traverse from **Lows Lake**. When we did this, we had the upper river to ourselves. Coming downstream, we bumped into many families of mergansers that entertained us with their dance on the water. Belted Kingfishers nest in the river's cut banks, and they would fly ahead of us, giving a clattering rattle. I was blown away by a bird I saw one morning as we were camping far above High Falls: a singing cardinal! It must not have found its summer home yet. Other birds that might be found along the river are Swamp, White-throated, and Lincoln's Sparrows, Alder and Least Flycatchers, and Northern Parula. Paddlers should consult *Adirondack Canoe Waters: North Flow*, published by the Adirondack Mountain Club. Another good resource for both canoeists and hikers is the Old Forge/Oswegatchie map published by National Geographic.

I've visited many places in the Five Ponds Wilderness, but I sure haven't seen it all, so I'm looking forward to more exploration. A word of warning: in 1995, a windstorm blew over thousands of trees in the region, making off-trail travel difficult. Most birders will want to stick to the trails and waterways. **—GL**

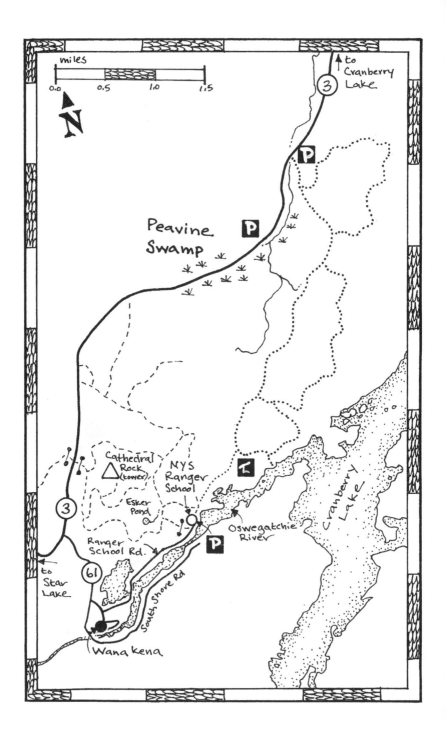

miles

0.0   0.5   1.0   1.5

N

to
Cranberry
Lake

3

P

Peavine
Swamp

P

Cathedral
Rock
(tower)

NYS
Ranger
School

Esker
Pond

3

Oswegatchie
River

Ranger
School Rd.

Cranberry
Lake

P

to
Star
Lake

61

South Shore Rd

Wana kena

25 Peavine Swamp

Pull off the highway to scan the swamp for Black-backed Woodpecker, Rusty Blackbird, and Yellow-bellied Flycatcher, among other birds. Woodland species can be found on a nearby trail that leads to the Oswegatchie River.

DIRECTIONS: From Cranberry Lake, drive west on NY 3. From the bridge over the Oswegatchie River, it's 1.2 miles to the parking lot for the Peavine Swamp Trail on the left. If you want to bird the swamp directly from the highway, continue driving west a short distance. The swamp is on both sides of the highway for the next few miles. To reach the New York State Ranger School in Wanakena, drive about five miles beyond the parking lot to County 61, turn left, and then follow the signs.

The state maintains about a dozen miles of hiking and cross-country ski trails that start from the Peavine Swamp parking lot. The main trail leads 4.1 miles through a beautiful hardwood forest to a lean-to on a stillwater section of the Oswegatchie River (it's really an arm of Cranberry Lake here). There are three loops off the main trail. The trail network lies a little east of Peavine Swamp. To see the swamp itself, most birders will want to stop along Route 3 west of the parking lot. Most of the swamp lies to the south. Much birding can be done from the road.

Boreal species found in and around the swamp include Black-backed Woodpecker, Rusty Blackbird, and Olive-sided and Yellow-bellied Flycatchers. Other birds you might encounter are Purple Finch, Cedar Waxwing, Alder Flycatcher, Swamp Sparrow, White-throated Sparrow, Red-breasted Nuthatch,

Peavine Swamp along State Route 3

Golden-crowned Kinglet, Northern Parula, and Nashville and Canada Warblers. Ospreys have a nest north of Route 3, visible from the road.

If you hike the trails, you'll see a nice stand of black cherry in the first mile. After that you'll be among the typical northern hardwoods—beech, yellow birch, and maple—with a few hemlock and red spruce. I have come across birch and red maple whose cut stumps measure four feet in diameter. Large boulders left behind by the last glacier are scattered along the trails. I have seen tracks of snowshoe hare, deer, bear, and coyote on the trail—and heard the coyotes cranking it up. I also have found Barred Owl feathers, but the raptors never answered my owl calls. I did see Scarlet Tanager, Rose-breasted Grosbeak, White-throated Sparrow, Hairy and Downy Woodpeckers, and a few warblers.

Another place to visit is the property owned by the New York State Ranger School in Wanakena. I did some good birding here along the network of dirt roads, seeing several wood warblers, Hermit and Swainson's Thrushes, Hairy and Downy Woodpeckers, and both nuthatches. In August 1999, I saw White-rumped Sandpipers by Esker Pond, which is on the school property. The land contains large softwood plantations where in good cone years you can find Pine Siskin and Red and White-winged Crossbills in winter. **—GL**

Illustration by Mike Storey

Cedar Waxwings

26 Massawepie Mire

Walk a dusty rail bed that cuts through the biggest bog in the Adirondacks. It's one of the best places in the state to look for the endangered Spruce Grouse, not to mention other boreal species such as Lincoln's Sparrow and Palm Warbler.

DIRECTIONS: From Tupper Lake, drive west on NY 3 toward Cranberry Lake for about 11 miles. Just past the sign for Gale, turn left into the Massawepie Boy Scout Reservation. Follow the dirt road 3.6 miles to a four-way intersection, reached after driving through the reservation. Turn right and go 0.2 miles to a Y intersection. Turn right again to reach a barrier in another 0.1 miles. This is the start of the walk up an old rail bed, but given the narrowness of the road, you may want to park near the Y intersection.

The Massawepie Mire is the biggest bog in the Adirondacks and one of the region's best birding locales. You can view the mire by walking along an old rail bed (later converted to a logging road) that is owned by the state. To drive to the rail bed, you must pass through the Massawepie Boy Scout Reservation. The Scouts enjoy exclusive use of the reservation from June 15 through August 31, but the road is open to the public year-round.

The road in becomes passable again in mid-May. You can walk for about two miles through the mire. The land on either side is private, so you must stay within fifty feet of the bed's centerline. But don't worry: you can see most of the birds right from the trail.

As you might guess, the mire is a hatchery for blackflies and mosquitoes, so be prepared. The few Tree Swallow boxes along the way aren't enough to take care of the bugs.

This has always been a good place to see Spruce Grouse, whose numbers are dwindling in New York State. Sometimes you come across them dusting in the railroad bed. They are a reclusive bird, but if you happen upon one, it will sit still and let you walk past, not making a sound.

Because the owners log the woods, the habitat is always changing. It's good for some birds, such as the Mourning Warbler and Philadelphia Vireo. Several other wood warblers can be heard along the rail bed. The boreal species most often seen and heard are Palm Warbler and Lincoln's

Sign on the road to Massawepie Mire

Photo by Phil Brown

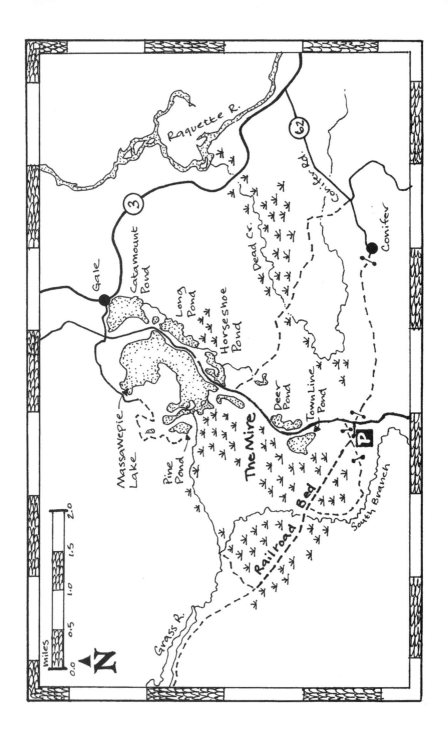

Spruce Grouse sometimes dust themselves in the old rail bed.

Photo by Phil Brown

Sparrow. Back in the 1980s, only one or two pairs of Palm Warblers inhabited the bog. In 2007, twenty-three males were heard singing one day, many within ten feet of the trail. These pretty warblers are one of the first to return and nest in the spring. Other boreal birds include Gray Jay, Black-backed Woodpecker, Rusty Blackbird, Boreal Chickadee, Nashville Warbler, and Olive-sided and Yellow-bellied Flycatchers. Just walking the trail brings most of these curious birds out to see who's in their woods. Lincoln's, Swamp, and Savannah Sparrows sing in the open bog areas.

In the alder beds along the brooks you can find Alder and Least Flycatchers, but you won't hear either singing until late May. Other warblers along the trail are Yellow-rumped, Chestnut-sided, Magnolia, Canada, Common Yellowthroat, Redstart, and Ovenbird.

Don't overlook the road you drove in. There are plenty of good birds along the way and around the nearby ponds. So many that you may never reach the mire! **—GL**

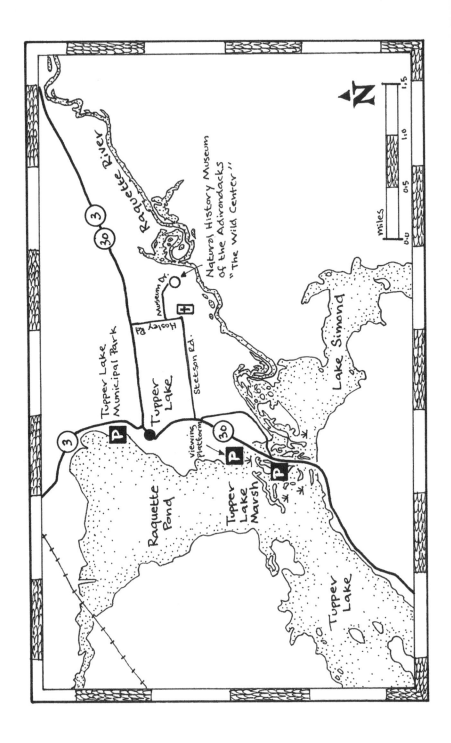

27 Tupper Lake Marsh & Municipal Park

Scan the vast marsh where the Raquette River meets Tupper Lake, looking for waterbirds such as Ring-necked Duck, Pied-billed Grebe, Wilson's Snipe, and Common Moorhen. Rare visitors include Trumpeter Swan, Sandhill Crane, and Northern Hawk Owl.

DIRECTIONS: From the intersection of NY 3 and NY 30 (at the Stewart's Shop) in Tupper Lake village, follow NY 3 west (actually northward here) toward Piercefield. The Municipal Park, with ballfield and parking, is in the open area on the left at the bottom of the hill. To reach the Tupper Lake Marsh, return to the Stewart's Shop intersection and follow NY 30 south toward Long Lake to the causeway that passes over the marsh. Park in one of the pull-offs. To reach the Natural History Museum of the Adirondacks (a k a the Wild Center), return to the Stewart's Shop and continue straight (east) on NY 3/30 to Hosley Avenue on the right. The entrance to the museum is a short way down Hosley, on the left.

Tupper Lake has a long history as a birding destination. When the Passenger Pigeon nested here in 1853, Samuel H. Hammond reported, "Hundreds of thousands of pigeons had flown away that morning, and yet there were hundreds of thousands, and perhaps many millions, old and young, there yet. It covered acres and acres—I have no idea how many, for I did not go around it." Although the Passenger Pigeon is sadly gone, the village's Municipal Park and Tupper Lake Marsh continue to attract birders, who have observed some remarkable birds. Birders also should consider a visit to the Natural History Museum of the Adirondacks, which opened in 2006.

The Municipal Park provides a good vantage to look for waterfowl on Raquette Pond, the northern arm or bay of Tupper Lake. A spotting scope may help in identifying Blue-winged and Green-winged Teals, Canvasback, Greater and Lesser Scaups, Long-tailed Duck, or other ducks that stop off during spring or fall migration. Ruddy Duck has been found on Raquette Pond several times over the years, as recently as late fall 1995. Sort among the local Canada Geese and migrant ducks for a Red-throated Loon, Red-necked Grebe, or Double-crested Cormorant. During May and from midsummer into fall, the shoreline of the park may attract shorebirds: not only "peeps" (including Western Sandpiper), but perhaps Semipalmated Plover, both yellowlegs, White-rumped Sandpiper, or Dunlin. Pay attention to the gulls: Bonaparte's Gull shows up in April and May and again in August, Little Gull has been found twice (three on July 9, 1997, and six on the ice November 9, 1992), and even a Black-headed Gull turned up April 19-21, 2003. Three Caspian Tern were found here July 10, 1997, and Common Tern shows up in summer. Sparrows favor the extensive open area, and flocks of Horned Lark or American Pipit stop off in migration.

Tupper Lake Marsh can be scanned from the Route 30 causeway just south of the village limits. Check the marsh for breeding Ring-necked Duck or Pied-billed Grebe. In winter look for Bald Eagle feeding on deer kills on the ice. The main lake is to the west, with Lake Simond and the Raquette River to the east. Canoeing the marsh and nearby Lake Simond—actually another bay of Tupper Lake—is best, but walking along the highway could also turn up a Common Moorhen, Wilson's Snipe, or singing Marsh Wren. This large cattail marsh, one of the best wetlands in the Adirondack Park, had a small colony of Black Tern until the 1980s, now extirpated due to aerial spraying of insecticide. Tupper Lake has records of Trumpeter Swan (2006), Western Grebe (1978), American White Pelican (1969), Cattle Egret (1976, 1983, 1985), Sandhill Crane (2005), and Northern Hawk Owl (1964, 1965, 1969, 1991), so expect anything. The marsh also can be scanned from a viewing platform built in 2008 north of the causeway.

You should allow time to visit the Natural History Museum (or Wild Center), where a trail leads down to two observation platforms overlooking the Oxbow on the Raquette River. Osprey fish in the museum's pond. Other species that might be seen at the museum include Bald Eagle, Belted Kingfisher, and Canada Goose. —JP

The new observation platform at Tupper Marsh

㉘ Floodwood Road

Stop at a series of attractive ponds and bogs along a forest road to check for Common Loon, Black-backed Woodpecker, Olive-sided and Alder Flycatchers, Northern Parula, and Northern Waterthrush. Blackpoll Warbler may be present in conifers.

DIRECTIONS: From the stoplight next to the town hall in Saranac Lake, drive north on NY 3 (Broadway). At the next light, NY 3 turns right, but you want to continue straight on NY 86 for about 4.5 miles to the T-intersection at Donnelly's Corners. Turn left onto NY 186 and continue straight for a little more than 9 miles, passing Lake Clear, the state fish hatchery, and the Saranac Inn Golf Course, to Floodwood Road on the right (you're close when you see the golf course). Shortly after the turn, bear left at a Y-intersection. From here, follow the road about 4 miles to East Pine Pond, just past the railroad tracks.

Floodwood Road, though mostly dirt, is well-maintained and provides easy access to birds. It passes a lovely series of headwater ponds of the Saranac River and crosses several small brooks with boggy openings. The forest includes stretches of quite mature and well-spaced hardwoods, as well as white pine and other conifers, especially around ponds. More than seventy-five species of woodland birds, including at least fifteen different warblers, nest in the vicinity. The lightly traveled road is used mostly by canoeists and fishermen, and there are endless places to pull over and bird. The original inn, located across Route 30 at the north end of Upper Saranac Lake, was called the Prospect House when it opened in 1864; the name was changed to Saranac Inn after its sale in 1886.

Shortly after passing the golf course, look for a rough dirt lane on the left that leads to Green Pond, which lies just north of Follensby Clear Pond. You can walk or drive to the shore to look and listen for birds. Afterward, continue on Floodwood Road to Polliwog Pond, the next body of water on the left. If Common Loon is not found here, there may be a pair on Middle or Floodwood Pond. Also check the bog pocket and small kettle pond on the right for Black-backed Woodpecker, and do the same at similar boggy areas farther along the road. Any of these wet areas may have Olive-sided and Alder Flycatchers, Veery, Northern Parula, Northern Waterthrush, or Swamp Sparrow. Although the elevation is only 1,600 feet, Blackpoll Warbler can occur in areas with conifers. Continue another mile to the next pond on the left, Middle Pond, and again look and listen for loons. Also be alert for Osprey, Bald Eagle, or Merlin around ponds, and a Broad-winged Hawk may flush in front of an approaching vehicle and glide ahead through the tunnel of trees. The entire eight-mile round trip also offers an excellent opportunity to encounter Adirondack mammals such as black bear, fisher, river otter, and white-tailed deer.

Just beyond Middle Pond, a trail on the right leads a half-mile to Long Pond in the St. Regis Canoe Area. After another mile the road crosses railroad tracks at Floodwood, once a stop on the Adirondack Division of the Penn-Central Railroad (and now the site of a store run by St. Regis Canoe Outfitters). Just beyond the crossing and Floodwood Pond there is another trail on the right leading to Long Pond. Either of the two side trails to Long Pond provides the opportunity for some exercise and the chance of spotting a few new Adirondack species. Continue driving to East Pine Pond on the left and yet another bog pocket on the right. About a mile beyond the tracks, a spur road on the right leads to a parking lot and the start of a short portage trail to the southwest arm of Long Pond. Just ahead on Floodwood Road a locked gate is reached, marking the end of public access. Most birders end their trip at East Pine Pond. Rather than birding on the inbound trip, some drive nonstop to East Pine to acquaint themselves with the route, then make a more leisurely return trip to Green Pond and Route 30. **—JP**

Photo by Phil Brown

Floodwood Road near Middle Pond

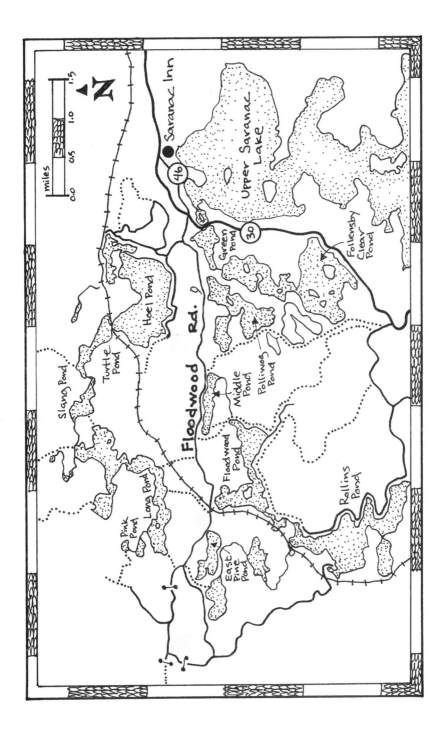

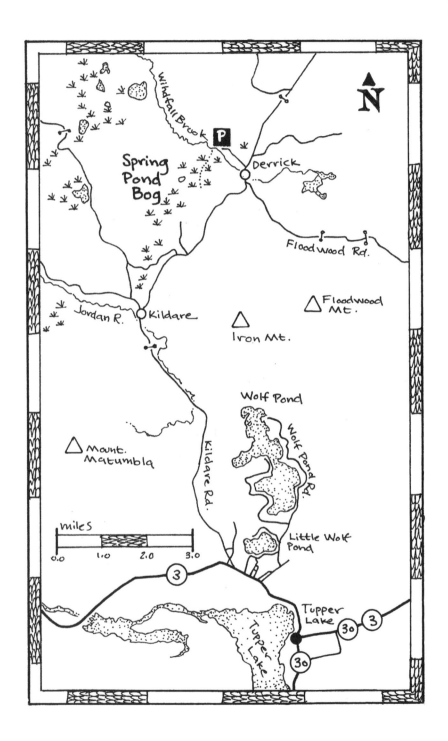

29 Spring Pond Bog

If you want to add the Spruce Grouse to your life list, ask the Nature Conservancy for permission to visit this preserve. It's one of your best bets for finding the rare bird. In all, more than 130 species have been observed here.

DIRECTIONS: Permission from the Adirondack Nature Conservancy is needed to visit this preserve, which is surrounded by private land. For a pass, call 518-576-2082 or e-mail Adirondacks@tnc.org. Access is via Kildare Road, a gated dirt road. From the junction of NY 3 and NY 30 in Tupper Lake, drive west on NY 3. On the edge of town, turn right onto Haymeadow Road (0.8 miles after crossing the railroad tracks). Take the first left onto Kildare Road, reached after a few hundred feet. Follow Kildare Road for about 5 miles to a gatehouse, where you must show your pass. Continue another 5 miles or so to the trailhead (see map). Free leaflets are available at the trailhead.

Spring Pond Bog is the second-largest open peatland in New York State. The bog mat itself covers five hundred acres. The entire preserve is 4,200 acres. The 0.3-mile trail follows an esker that extends into the bog. There is a small spur trail with a boardwalk that goes out over the bog mat. Don't leave the trails and roads when birding in the preserve.

More than 130 species have been observed here, including such boreal species as Spruce Grouse, Black-backed and American Three-toed Woodpeckers, Gray Jay, Boreal Chickadee, Olive-sided and Yellow-bellied Flycatchers, Tennessee and Palm Warblers, and Short-eared Owl. The preserve is one of the best places in the state for seeing Spruce Grouse, as they dust in and along the dirt roads. There are three or four breeding pairs on

The boardwalk at Spring Pond Bog

the property. Palm Warblers have nested for years at the end of the esker trail. The other boreal species can be found just about anywhere along the trails and roads.

You never know what you might see in this habitat. In 2000, I walked the entire bog while conducting research for the second edition of the state breeding-bird atlas. As I was getting back to the esker, I thought I heard Wild Turkeys. I took out my call, and sure enough three jakes came out on the bog mat toward me. That day, I saw all the boreal birds except Spruce Grouse and Short-eared Owl. I also saw a beautiful female Northern Harrier hunting over the bog. On another trip, with the Federation of New York State Bird Clubs (now the New York State Ornithological Association), we had Golden-winged Warbler singing along one of the roads. All of the wood warblers have been found here. If you're lucky, you might see a Bay-breasted or Cape May. The open bog mat also has breeding Vesper and Savannah Sparrows.

The dirt roads on the way to the preserve also are good for birding Common Loons nest on some of the ponds on private lands inside the gate. For boreal species, take a walk on the roads west of the bog. You might find Spruce Grouse nesting in this area. Look for dusting spots and scat. Ruffed Grouse also live in the vicinity, so if you see a grouse, it's not necessarily a Spruce. This endangered bird also has been observed in the spruce-tamarack habitat in the half-mile before the Kildare Road gate. **—GL**

Wild Turkey

30 St. Regis Canoe Area

Paddle the delightful Seven Carries while looking for some of the seventy-five species of birds that dwell here. You could see Common Goldeneye, Black-backed Woodpecker, Ruby-crowned Kinglet, or another of the boreal birds. And loons.

DIRECTIONS: Canoes or kayaks may be launched at several sites: The Black Pond parking area on Keese Mill Road, about 2.5 miles west of NY 3 (and Paul Smith's College); the landing at Upper Saint Regis, on St. Regis Carry road, reached from NY 3 about 3.5 miles south of the college; and the state parking lot on Little Clear Pond, reached from Fish Hatchery Road, just east of Saranac Inn off NY 3. A good resource is *Adirondack Canoe Waters: North Flow*, published by the Adirondack Mountain Club. Also bring a topographical map. All or part of the Seven Carries can be done as a day trip, but an overnight in the Canoe Area will permit more exploration and is recommended. The route may be followed in either direction.

The route of the Seven Carries was a popular guideboat trip in the late nineteenth century, when vacationers would travel between Paul Smith's Hotel and Saranac Inn. Camp owners and guests also traveled the route through Spitfire Lake to attend services at one of two churches in Paul Smiths: St. John's in the Wilderness and St. Regis Presbyterian. Today the 18,200-acre St. Regis Canoe Area provides access to fifty-eight wild lakes and ponds free of motorized watercraft and offers the birder over seventy-five species of Adirondack birds. Most will be the more common species, but an encounter with a Common Goldeneye, Black-backed Woodpecker, Ruby-crowned Kinglet, or other boreal bird is always a possibility. Common Loons may be seen on several of the ponds.

From the Black Pond parking lot, take a few extra minutes to hike or paddle the short distance to lovely Black Pond, which may have nesting Common Loons. After returning to the lot, launch across the road and paddle east along the channel to Lower Saint Regis Lake, with Paul Smith's College visible on the left. Keep right and enter the Slew, a wide marshy stream that leads into Spitfire Lake, watching for bitterns and other wetland birds. At Spitfire, the first Merlin nest with young in New York State was found in a spruce above the shoreline camps in 1992. Cross the lake to tiny Rabbit Island, where Dr. Edward Livingston Trudeau quarantined animals for experiments with the tubercle bacillus, and enter the larger Upper Saint Regis Lake with its elegant camps and boathouses (often storing guideboats, mahogany speedboats, and antique Idem sailboats), not to mention the lake's nesting loons.

After rounding a large island with camps and passing several smaller islands, look for the Upper Saint Regis dock. Paddle to the right (west), staying

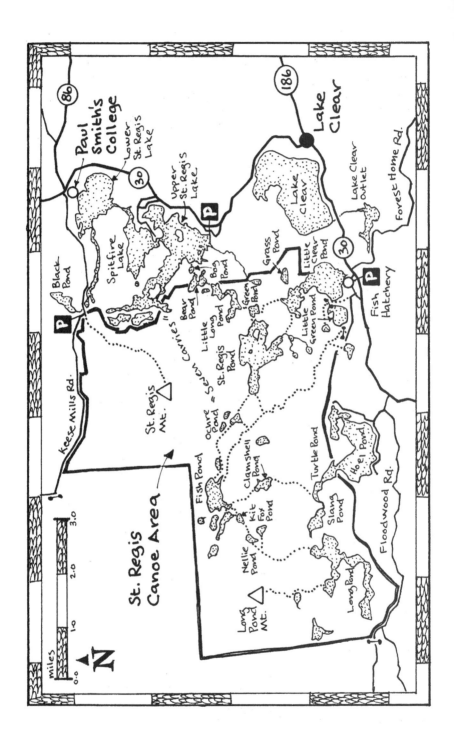

Photo by Phil Brown

On the route of the Seven Carries

close to shore, and watch for a small sign on a tree marking the first short portage, or carry, into minuscule Bog Pond (unnamed on the topo map), whose water is brown from tannin. Another short portage leads to Bear Pond, its milky blue water exhibiting an astonishing clarity. Common Goldeneye hens with broods were found here in the late 1970s. A third carry leads to Little Long Pond, where a hen goldeneye was found in 1984. Located at 1,654 feet, Little Long marks the drainage of the Middle Branch of the St. Regis River. Pass through the narrows to the far shore and take the fourth portage to aptly named Green Pond. Paddle west across this small pond and make the extremely brief fifth portage into St. Regis Pond, where a Bonaparte's Gull was seen in July 1977.

St. Regis Pond, one of the largest waterbodies in the Canoe Area, is an excellent pond for an overnight, but all or most of the campsites may be occupied in midsummer. After reaching the pond, explore the tiny bog pond just to the south. Then round the peninsula and follow the southern channel to the sixth and longest portage (0.6 miles) to Little Clear Pond, which also has loons. Cross the pond to the parking lot on the southwestern shore. A seventh carry to Little Green Pond is usually skipped. Leaving a second vehicle at Little Clear Pond avoids the return paddle to Black Pond (or vice versa). The trip can be shortened by starting or ending at Upper St. Regis Lake instead of Black Pond.

If camping at St. Regis Pond, take the time to hike (or carry) to Ochre, Clamshell, Bessie, Nellie, Kit Fox, Fish, Little Fish, Little Long, and Lydia ponds to the west. Each waterbody has its own charm, and Kit Fox and this Little Long (smaller than the other) had hen goldeneyes in August 1984 and may well still. **—JP**

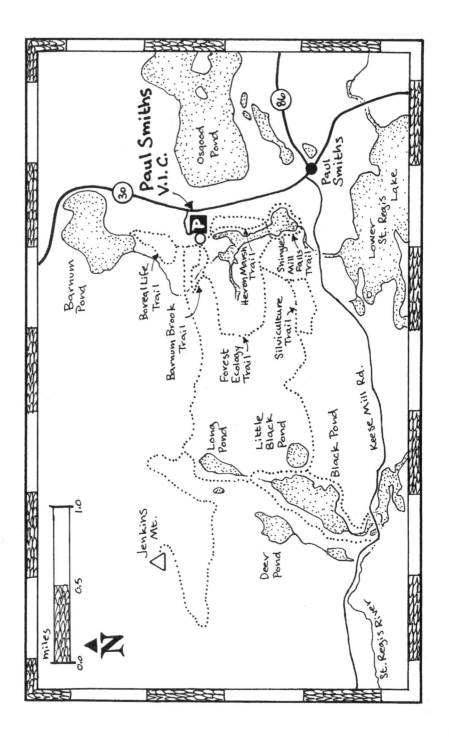

31 **Paul Smiths Visitor Interpretive Center**

Take your pick of several well-maintained trails at a state-run nature center. Most birders start with the Boreal Life Trail, with its long boardwalk through a bog and spruce swamp. It also offers an elevated platform for observing waterfowl on Barnum Pond.

DIRECTIONS: From the intersection of NY 30 and NY 86 in Paul Smiths (near the entrance to Paul Smith's College), drive north on NY 30 for a mile and turn left at the sign for the state-run Visitor Interpretive Center. Trail maps are available at the center and online at www.adkvic.org.

The state's Adirondack Park Agency operates two Visitor Interpretive Centers, one in Paul Smiths in the northern lake belt, the other in Newcomb south of the High Peaks. Both house natural-history exhibits and offer trails for hiking and skiing. The Paul Smiths VIC (pronounced "Vick") boasts 2,885 acres containing nearly all types of habitat found in the Park. Most of the property is boreal forest, providing easy access to a wide variety of northern birds, but the site also features other forest types. Wetlands include five ponds, several brooks, bogs, fens, swamps, and the sixty-acre Heron Marsh. Black, Little Black, and Long ponds are most easily reached, on foot or by canoe, from Keese Mill Road west of Paul Smith's College. Black Pond often has Common Loon, and both Barred and Northern Saw-whet Owls call there after dark, sometimes in counterpoint with the loons.

This VIC has six miles of interpretive trails, with signage, and eight miles of backcountry trails. The half-dozen interpretive trails, originating at the visitor building, are Barnum Brook (0.8 miles), Boreal Life (1.3 miles), Forest Ecology (1.2 miles), Heron Marsh (0.8 miles), Shingle Mill Falls (0.7 miles), and Silviculture (0.9 miles). Each has its merits, but most birders favor the Boreal Life Trail (yellow markers), featuring a 1,600-foot boardwalk through a spruce swamp and boreal bog. At its start, the trail passes through an upland conifer forest of balsam fir, tamarack (eastern larch), spruces, white pine, and hemlock, reaching a giant pine and then turning left toward Barnum Pond. An elevated overlook tower provides scenic views of the pond and Jenkins and St. Regis mountains. Scan the sky for soaring raptors and the shoreline marshes for Wood Duck, American Black Duck, Ring-necked Duck, American Bittern, Great Blue Heron, and other wetland birds. Leaving Barnum Pond, the trail soon crosses the long boardwalk that traverses the swamp and bog. Black-backed Woodpecker nests

A birder checks out Heron Marsh at the VIC.

nearby and is often seen in this area. The "Yellow" subspecies of Palm Warbler (*D.p. hypochrysea*) was first confirmed as a breeding species in New York State in 1984, with the discovery of a nest on Bay Pond Bog, about six miles to the west. During the decades that followed, "Yellow" Palms were seen on other Adirondack bogs, with the first singing males found at the Paul Smiths VIC on April 28, 2003. Since then, they've nested annually near Barnum Brook. During late June and early July the bog erupts with the blooms of native orchids: grass-pink, rose pogonia, and a sea of white fringed orchis. After the boardwalk, the forest changes to hardwoods. Take a left on Jenkins Mountain Road to loop back to the center.

Barnum Brook Trail (red markers) follows the brook on a boardwalk; Forest Ecology Trail (orange markers) has a nine-hundred-foot boardwalk across a peatland; Heron Marsh Trail (green markers) has two boardwalks and a tower, and Shingle Mill Falls Trail (blue markers) features a three-hundred-foot pontoon bridge across a marsh. All offer good birding, but it's tough to do them all in a day. Most birders leave with plans to revisit the Paul Smiths VIC. The Silviculture Trail (yellow markers) loops through plantation pines off the Forest Ecology Trail and is perhaps the least promising route for birding. —**JP**

32 Madawaska

Walk on a former tote road past the nesting grounds of several northern species as well as a number of warblers. Another option is to paddle Madawaska Pond, where you could see Green-Winged Teal, American Bittern, or a Bald Eagle.

DIRECTIONS: Western approach: From Paul Smiths, turn west from NY 30 onto Keese Mill Road. Go 6 miles west to a gate, where the road turns right, becoming Blue Mountain Road (which ends at NY 458 south of St. Regis Falls). Continue another 6 miles on Blue Mountain Road to a DEC parking area on the left. Walk back a short distance to the gate on the opposite (east) side, the start of a sandy tote road (closed to vehicles). **Northeastern approach:** From NY 30 at the south end of Meacham Lake, turn west onto NY 458, proceeding downhill just over a mile to a state Forest Preserve sign and gravel road on the left. Follow this road a half-mile and turn left at the Madawaska sign. Continue 5 miles and turn left at a T-intersection. Park at the new DEC parking area among tall pines near Madawaska Pond.

Long considered the premier boreal birding site in the Adirondacks, much of the Madawaska region was added to the state-owned Forest Preserve in 1999, providing public access to lands formerly owned by Champion International. The purchase also opened a new route to Madawaska Pond from the northeast.

Nevertheless, access problems remain. For over a half-century, birders approached Madawaska Pond from the west, after obtaining permission from the Madawaska Club, sometimes paying a modest fee for an entrance card. They followed a tote road a mile and a half to an old railroad bed, then turned left to follow the bed to the pond. In the Champion deal, however, another hunting club bought the railroad bed. As of 2008, the club did not allow public access on the bed. This means hikers coming from the west cannot reach the pond unless they bushwhack across state land.

This is not as bad as it seems, for plenty of birding can be done along the tote road. Also, the drive to the western trailhead offers ten miles of good birding. Just after the right turn at the Rockefeller gate, the road enters the Brandon Burn, a forty-thousand-acre tract that burned in 1903. Over a century later there are large expanses of blueberry barrens and even a few charred stumps. Watch for Eastern Bluebird and other open-country species, perhaps even a Common Nighthawk perched in daytime. The little-traveled road crosses the Middle Branch of the St. Regis, then passes through stretches of excellent spruce-balsam habitat. Pull over where convenient to look for boreal birds. Just reaching the Madawaska gate can take a while, the temptation to stop and bird being so great. (Good birding can also be found farther north along the road near Quebec Brook.)

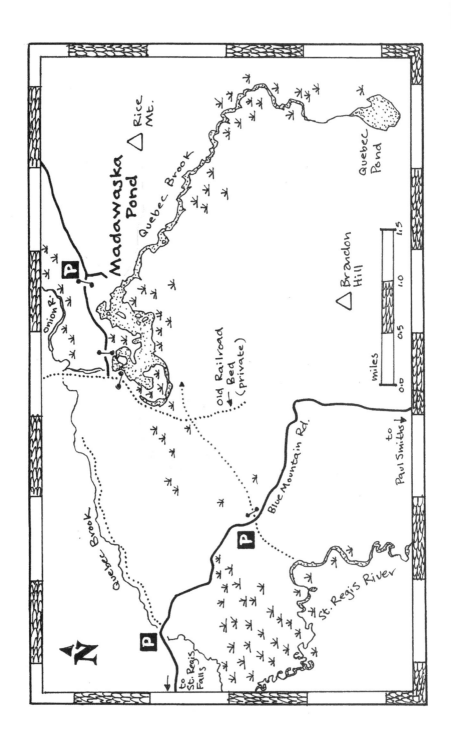

Photo by Phil Brown

Madawaska Pond

The DEC parking area is at the start of a 0.7-mile canoe carry to the Middle Branch of the St. Regis River. Before entering the Madawaska tract, walk down the carry a few hundred feet to a bog pond on the left. Common Goldeneye, Ring-necked Duck, and other waterfowl have been seen there.

Return to the parking area and cross the road to reach the Madawaska gate. The tote road passes over three low rises en route to the railroad bed, the third known as a spot to find Spruce Grouse during the last half of the twentieth century. The fool hens may now be extirpated, but this is still a good stretch of boreal forest to find Black-backed Woodpecker, Yellow-bellied and Olive-sided Flycatchers, Gray Jay, and Boreal Chickadee, along with a variety of warblers. In years with a bumper crop of cones, this is also a good stretch for finding boreal finches, with Red Crossbills and flocks of White-winged Crossbills present in August 2008. After a half-mile, the habitat changes to fairly dense white pine, some with loose slabs of bark used by nesting Brown Creepers. Near the intersection with the rail bed, the habitat becomes boreal again. Don't be surprised to see moose tracks on the way in.

Nearly all birders will want to turn around at the intersection, but it is legal to cross the rail bed and bushwhack across state land to Madawaska Pond. Just after crossing the bed, turn left into the woods and head north to northeast. Be sure to bring a map and compass.

The easiest way to see Madawaska Pond is to drive to the new parking lot from Route 458. From there, it's a short walk to the water. You may want to bring a spotting scope to check for ducks or loons. Better yet, explore the water by canoe or kayak. The pond may have Green-winged Teal, among other waterfowl, in summer. Be sure to scrutinize the small dead snags in case one might transmogrify into an American Bittern, neck pointing skyward. Virginia Rail might be prompted to answer from the brushy shorelines. In wetlands near the rail bed, listen for Olive-Sided and Alder Flycatchers. Bald Eagle (and occasionally a Golden) might be seen at Madawaska. —**JP**

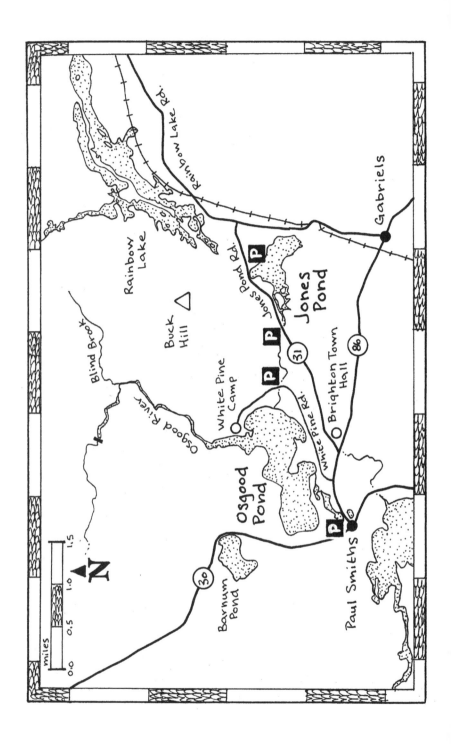

Jones & Osgood Ponds

Take a delightful canoe trip through extensive boreal habitat and look for both American Three-toed and Black-backed Woodpeckers, Ring-necked Duck, Palm Warbler, and Gray Jay

DIRECTIONS: There are three put-ins, two along Jones Pond Road and one along White Pine Road. Directions for all are given from the junction of NY 86 and County 60 (Rainbow Lake Road) in Gabriels, a hamlet that lies between Saranac Lake and Paul Smiths. To reach Jones Pond Road, head north on County 60 for 2 miles to Jones Pond Road (County 31) and turn left. Go 0.6 miles to a put-in on the left at Jones Pond or 1.5 miles to a bridge over the pond's outlet. For the third put-in, drive west on NY 86 from the Gabriels junction for 3.1 miles to White Pine Road and turn right. Go 1.5 miles to another bridge over the Jones Pond outlet. The optional Church Pond take-out on NY 86 is 0.7 miles west of White Pine Road.

Few canoe trips in the Adirondacks are as pleasant or offer as much variety in a few hours as the paddle from Jones Pond to Osgood Pond and the Osgood River. Many birders put in and take out at White Pine Road to shorten the excursion, but if you have the time, it's recommended that you put in at Jones Pond and take out at Church Pond, though this requires a car shuttle or bicycle to get back to your starting point.

If you do begin at Jones, in ten or fifteen minutes you'll reach the outlet, which winds past a large marsh and black spruce/tamarack swamp. Many kinds of duck, including Ring-necked, can be found here, along with Great Blue and Green Herons, American and Least Bitterns, and various warblers. You may want to explore the marsh's side channels.

After the marsh, the outlet flows under a highway bridge (about a mile from the put-in) and enters more forested habitat. Black-backed Woodpecker nests near the bridge and farther downstream in areas of standing dead timber. Gray Jay also inhabits this stretch. About a mile from the first bridge, the shallow stream passes under White Pine Road. In the quarter-mile between here and Osgood Pond, listen attentively for warblers. A Bald Eagle often perches on a tree near the outlet's mouth.

Once on Osgood Pond, head diagonally to the right (northwest) toward a small building on a point. This is the Japanese Tea House at the historic White Pine Camp. Built in 1907-08, White Pine Camp served as the "Summer White House" for President Coolidge in 1926. It now is a resort open to the public. When crossing the pond, keep alert for Merlin and Common Loon, both of which nest nearby. Shortly after passing the tea-house, you'll reach the Osgood River. You can paddle more than two and a half miles down the Osgood, as far as an old log dam. For much of the way, the river is bordered by boreal habitat—a black spruce/tamarack swamp

The Japanese Tea House at White Pine Camp

and a sedge mat that resembles Canadian muskeg.

American Three-toed Woodpecker has been seen along the first mile of the river, but the Black-backed is much more common and can be found more often than not. Palm Warbler nests in the bog on the west side. Other warblers include Nashville, Magnolia, Northern Parula, Black-throated Blue, and Black-throated Green. Boreal Chickadee, Lincoln's and Swamp Sparrows, and both kinglets also are around. In years of good cone crops, look for Red and White-winged Crossbills. Broad-winged Hawk often soars above the river. You also may want to explore Blind Brook, an alder-lined tributary that comes in from the east where the river swings west.

If you decide to take out at Church Pond, after passing the teahouse on the return trip, head southwest to round a large point, entering a bay on the southern shore. In the southwest corner of the bay, take a tiny canal to Little Osgood Pond. About halfway across this small pond, turn left (south) into another canal, which leads to Church Pond, and take out at a dock on Route 86. These enchanting canals were dug by hand around 1900 so summer residents of Osgood Pond could row or paddle to church in Paul Smiths.

The trip is best done in late May or in June, when the birds are singing, but it is rewarding at any time, no matter which variation you prefer. By the way, those who don't have a canoe can bird the Jones Pond outlet from the bridge on Jones Pond Road. **—Phil Brown**

Bloomingdale Bog

Take a short walk down an old railroad bed to enter the world of the Gray Jay, Boreal Chickadee, and Black-backed Woodpecker. Other residents of this bog include Yellow-bellied Flycatcher, Ruby-crowned Kinglet, and Lincoln's Sparrow.

DIRECTIONS: Take NY 86 north from Saranac Lake, passing the turnoff to Lake Clear Junction and the Adirondack Airport on the left, and continue two more miles, passing the Harrietstown cemetery. Where the highway begins to curve left toward Gabriels, take County 55 to the east (right) toward Bloomingdale. This road soon enters a boreal corridor; after 1.75 miles watch for a pull-off on the right and a vehicle barrier at the start of the trail. See map, p. 133.

The Bloomingdale Bog is easily accessed by an old railroad grade that runs south from Onchiota to Lake Colby, just north of Saranac Lake. From Route 55, the grade can be followed a half-mile north to **Bigelow Road**, through some excellent northern habitat and wetlands where Black-backed Woodpecker nests. Most birders, however, follow the grade on the south side of the highway, which leads to the large bog. The rail bed provides firm, level walking when the ground is bare and excellent cross-country skiing in winter, although snowmobiles should be expected, especially on weekends, when snow covers the ground. Boreal birds may be observed as soon as you leave the car. A curious Gray Jay family may drift across the trail, hoping for a handout, or the nasal *chick-che-day-day* of a Boreal Chickadee may be heard in the thick tunnel of spruce-balsam that borders the rail grade. Be alert for the soft tapping of a Black-backed Woodpecker. American Three-toed Woodpecker has not been observed for many years but remains a possibility.

Just a quarter-mile in from the road, the grade crosses a major power line cut that runs parallel to Route 55. This large open area is a shrub swamp, filled with plants in the heath family that have leaves that retard evaporation. Look for

Photo by Jeff Nadler

Alder Flycatcher

bog laurel and bog rosemary, cranberry, Labrador tea, and leatherleaf, as well as the insectivorous sundew and pitcher plants. Listen for the snappy *fee-bee-o* of Alder Flycatcher in the speckled alders. Scan the sky above this wide opening for a soaring Broad-winged Hawk or other raptors. A

The Bloomingdale Bog

Northern Hawk Owl frequented this area from December 30, 2000, through March 19, 2001, entertaining countless visitors.

Past the power-line cut, the trailside habitat returns to black spruce-balsam fir, with the odd white spruce and a few stands of tamarack. During summer, Yellow-bellied Flycatcher, Ruby-crowned Kinglet, and Lincoln's Sparrow can be heard along the way and perhaps spished into sight. A series of bog pockets and wet areas provides openings and a scattering of northern shrubs. Check the tops of dead snags for Ruby-throated Hummingbird or Olive-sided Flycatcher. At least fifteen warblers occur here, with "Yellow" Palm Warbler found near the bog openings, but a Wilson's Warbler discovered in May 2004 apparently was a one-week wonder. A Sedge Wren was located on territory near one of the bog pockets in June 2001. A male Spruce Grouse was dusting in a sandy patch in June 2000 (scat of this species could be found to at least 2004). About a hundred species of birds nest in the vicinity, joined by migrants and winter visitants. From the power line, the trail continues three and a half miles through the bog to Route 86, but most birders walk just a half-mile or mile before turning back. Even without a hawk owl as an attraction, Bloomingdale Bog is an interesting area to bird in winter, especially in years marked by an invasion of crossbills or other winter finches. —JP

㉟ Bigelow Road

In summer, stroll down this dirt lane in search of any of the boreal birds, except Spruce Grouse. Come back in winter with snowshoes or skis to look for crossbills, Pine Siskin, Northern Shrike, and other visitors.

DIRECTIONS: From Saranac Lake, take NY 3 north along the Saranac River to Bloomingdale. At the stop sign in the hamlet, continue straight ahead, with Norman's Store on the right. As County 55 swings left (west) toward Bloomingdale Bog and Gabriels, veer right onto Oregon Plains Road. The road soon crosses Sumner Brook on a small concrete bridge. Continuing north, look for a dirt road on the left, a little more than a half-mile beyond the bridge. This is Bigelow Road. It's best to park at the start of the road and hike (or ski or snowshoe) the 1.5 miles to Negro Brook, where a bridge is out. Those coming from **Bloomingdale Bog** should take County 55 east to Bloomingdale, then turn left onto Oregon Plains Road.

Bigelow Road is a year-round destination for those in search of boreal birds, but it is especially popular in those winters when the region is invaded by nesting crossbills and other winter finches. Somewhat off the beaten track, Bigelow Road runs roughly parallel to the Route 55 boreal corridor but without the hazards and distractions of highway traffic. The habitat is largely spruce-balsam, with pockets of wetland and alder thickets, especially in the vicinities of Negro, Rickerson, and Twobridge brooks. This road is flat and easy to traverse. The only drawbacks may be blackflies, deerflies, or snowmobiles in season. A little more than a mile in, the road crosses an old railroad bed that runs south from Onchiota to Lake Colby. A side trip to the south, following the abandoned rail bed, leads in less than a mile to Route 55 and, across the highway, to the entrance to Bloomingdale Bog. Although less productive in summer, this option provides an interesting alternative to continuing on Bigelow Road and is a good cross-country ski leg in winter.

Most of the Adirondacks' boreal birds, with the exception of Spruce Grouse, can be found along Bigelow Road. Black-backed Woodpecker, Gray Jay, and Boreal Chickadee are present throughout the year, as is Common Raven. In summer, birders might also encounter Olive-sided, Yellow-bellied, and Alder Flycatchers, Ruby-crowned Kinglet, Cape May and Bay-breasted Warblers, Lincoln's Sparrow, and Rusty Blackbird. Both Red and White-winged Crossbills can occur in all months, but they are absent in some years and abundant in others, especially in winters with a bumper cone crop. During the invasion winter of 2006-07, neither crossbill was reported until December 31, but afterward both species were easily found into March. Some winters also see invasions of Northern Shrike, Red-breasted Nuthatch, Purple Finch, Pine Siskin, or American Goldfinch along the road or in Bloomingdale Bog.

Bigelow Road

Despite the popularity of Bigelow Road and Bloomingdale Bog, birders should not ignore the other superb birding opportunities in the vicinity of Bloomingdale, Onchiota, and Vermontville. From Route 3 in Bloomingdale, take River Road south and then east toward Franklin Falls for 1.5 miles, then turn right onto Moose Pond Road, crossing the Saranac River on a wooden bridge, continuing south on the gravel road to the pond. A small bog on the right had an active nest of Black-backed Woodpecker in July 2007. An informal trail continues around scenic Moose Pond. All the species at Bigelow Road can be found along Oregon Plains Road, especially within a half-mile of Bigelow. Taking Oregon Plains Road north to Onchiota, with side trips down Muzzy and Swinyer, also provides great birding. So do the roads surrounding "Onchi" and nearby Buck Pond. —**JP**

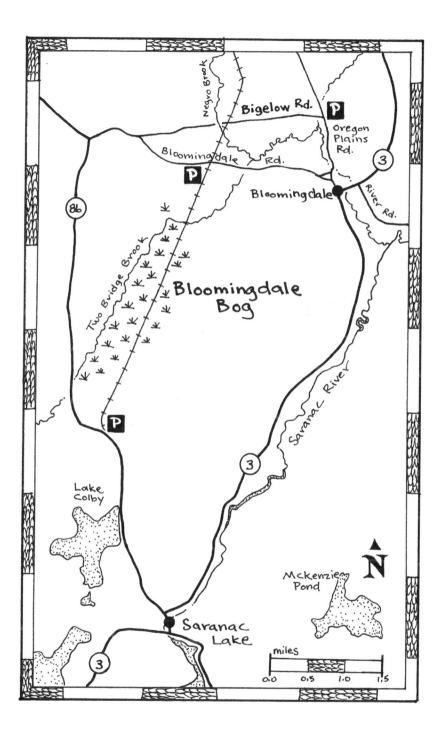

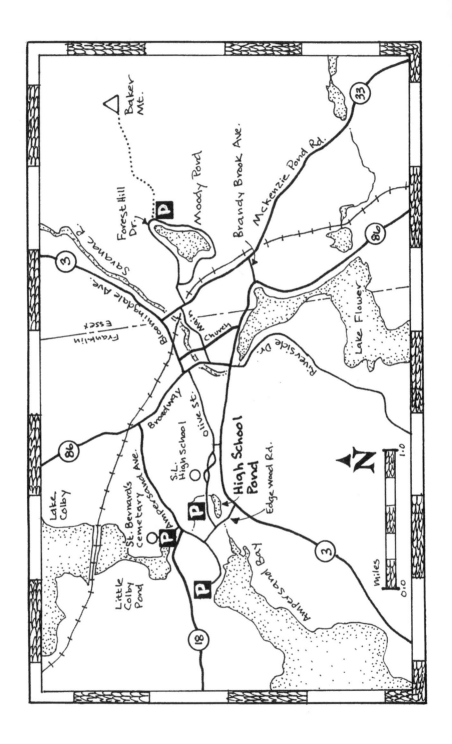

Saranac Lake Village

Check a small pond for such migrants as Solitary Sandpiper, Short-billed Dowitcher, and American Pipit. Breeding birds also frequent the area, including Northern Waterthrush and Northern Parula

DIRECTIONS: From the stoplight on NY 3 near the town hall in Saranac Lake village, drive west on NY 3 for 0.8 miles and turn right onto Edgewood Road. The pond will soon appear on the right.

The small pond at Saranac Lake High School is a good birding spot during spring and fall migrations. After ice-out, the pond attracts American Black Duck and other waterfowl. Shorebirds like Solitary Sandpiper sometimes turn up, with a flock of fourteen Short-billed Dowitchers a highlight in late May 2005. Walk along the inlet to see if any early Yellow-bellied or Alder Flycatchers have stopped at the alder thickets or if a Swamp Sparrow has arrived. As many as seventy-five American Pipits have been seen here in May. The woods should be checked for warbler arrivals. Northern Parula, Black-throated Green and Blackburnian Warblers, and Northern Waterthrush are a few of the species that might be around in early May, but rarities are possible. A Prairie Warbler turned up on May 5, 1999, but an even more exciting find was the first and only Worm-eating Warbler in Franklin County on April 30, 2004.

Puddle ducks like American Wigeon and Blue-winged Teal begin to return to the weedy pond in late September and October, with a Northern Pintail once lingering as late as December 29. Other wetland species such as Green Heron frequent the shoreline, along with southbound shorebirds like Pectoral Sandpiper and Wilson's Snipe. Mixed flocks of fall warblers are frequent, and the woods may have Great Crested Flycatcher into late September and Rose-breasted Grosbeak as late as early October. By winter the activity has died down, but as the late December pintail suggests, the pond is well worth checking until ice forms.

Take the first left off Edgewood Road for Ampersand Bay, where the first wayward Fish Crow was found at the boat launch on August 9, 1998. Farther up the road is St Bernard's Cemetery, a quiet oasis where flocks of passerine migrants stop to feed and rest. One of the county's few sightings of Orange-crowned Warbler was made here on October 20, 1996. Other birding sites in the village include Lake Flower and the Saranac River as it wends through downtown. Moody Pond on the east side of the village (see map) is also worth checking. As many as 140 Ring-necked Ducks gathered there in November 1993, and a nearby feeder hosted a rare Harris's Sparrow from October 27 to November 5, 1980. A mile-long trail up scenic Baker Mountain begins near Moody Pond. **—JP**

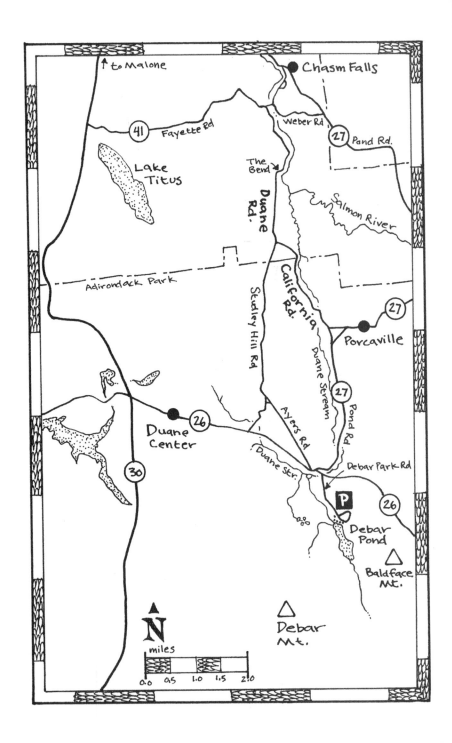

California Road & Debar Pond

Drive along a back road past habitat for Northern Waterthrush, Gray Jay, Black-backed Woodpecker, Swamp Sparrow, and a dozen species of warbler. Extend your birding expedition with a short walk to Debar Pond.

DIRECTIONS: From Chasm Falls, east of NY 30 and Lake Titus on County 41, take the Duane Road south along the Salmon River. At "The Bend," where the road leaves the river, continue south on the Duane Road 1.3 miles to California Road and turn left. Follow the road east, then south to County 26. Turn left and then take a quick right onto the access road to Debar Pond. Drive to the public parking area on the left.

Birders in search of an easy drive, with virtually no traffic, through prime spruce-fir boreal habitat—with a river and stream thrown in for good measure—should consider a visit to California Road in the northern Adirondacks, followed by a side trip to scenic Debar Pond. Driving south from Chasm Falls en route to California Road, there are several pull-offs where you can check the banks and waters of the Salmon River. Scan the sky for Broad-winged and Red-tailed Hawks. After the left turn onto California Road, the habitat quickly takes on a more northern flavor, and birders can stop and walk at any point along the five-mile seasonal dirt road. At the end of the eastward leg, Northern Waterthrush favors the wet woods where the road crosses tiny Tontine Brook. The road then curves right (south) through a mile-long corridor of tall conifers.

A dozen or more species of warblers may be heard or seen at the height of birdsong in June and early July, along with Blue-headed Vireo, Winter Wren, Swainson's Thrush, Purple Finch, and other forest birds. Listen for the buzzy *zeeeeeeeee-up!* song of Northern Parula in spruces festooned with old-man's-beard lichen. Be sure to stop along the stretch of blowdown areas on the west side, where openings and standing dead trees attract woodpeckers. Give a few Barred Owl calls, and Yellow-bellied Sapsuckers, Hairy Woodpeckers, or Black-backed Woodpeckers should soon appear to investigate. Whether Hairy or the desired three-toed species appears is a matter of luck, but as many as four Black-backed at a time were seen here in early July 2004, one a variant male with an orange (rather than yellow) crown patch. Be alert for the song or call of a Yellow-bellied Flycatcher. A curious family of Gray Jays may drift silently across the road to investigate voices or owl calls, always eager for a handout.

An increase in speckled alder along the west side of California Road indicates that Duane Stream is now running parallel to, but just out of sight of, the road. Begin to listen now for Alder Flycatcher and Swamp Sparrow.

Stop at the left curve and small bridge over the stream, where the opening may provide a view of an Olive-sided Flycatcher calling for *Free beer!* atop a dead snag, while Common Yellowthroats scold nearby. Passing by Run Road (which goes east to Porcaville), the road becomes known as Pond Road down to Route 26, with the habitat quickly reverting to mixed and hardwood forest before reaching the highway.

At Route 26, turn left, then take a quick right to reach DeBar Pond. From the public parking area, cross the dirt road to take the boardwalk trail to the pond, where a canoe or kayak may be launched. Black-backed Woodpecker occur along the access road between the highway and parking area and may even be found at the highway intersection itself. A return loop to Chasm Falls can be taken on the paved Duane (or Ayers) Road that runs parallel to California Road on the west. Obviously, this trip can also be done in reverse, beginning at Debar Pond and driving north on California Road. No matter the direction taken, the boreal birding should be both interesting and traffic-free. —**JP**

Plank walkway on the Debar Pond trail

West-Central Region

Woods and Waters of the Wild West

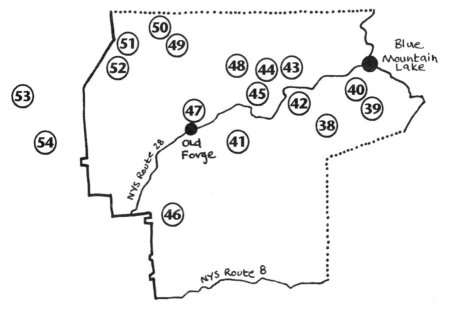

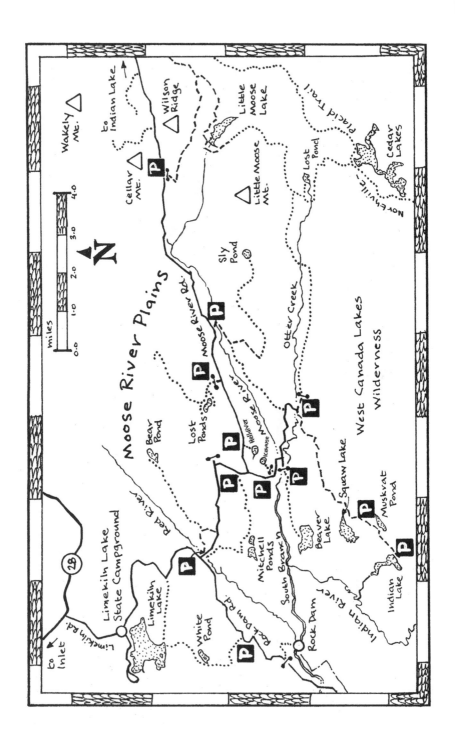

Moose River Plains

Go car camping in the Plains and spend a few days visiting all the sites where you can see interesting birds (and perhaps a moose). More than 150 avian species have been observed here, including the rare Spruce Grouse.

DIRECTIONS: The Moose River Plains Recreation Area has two entrances, connected by Moose River Road. For the western entrance, located east of Inlet, turn south from NY 28 onto Limekiln Lake Road and drive 2 miles. Just past the entrance to the Limekiln Lake State Campground, turn left onto Moose River Road. For the eastern entrance, located west of Indian Lake, turn southwest from NY 28/30 onto Cedar River Road and drive about 12 miles to the gatehouse near the **Cedar River Flow**.

The Moose River Plains Recreation Area is one of the most accessible places for birding in the Adirondacks. It has twenty-eight miles of dirt roads that will take you to most of the good birding habitats. The roads are open to motor vehicles from Memorial Day until the first Sunday in December. In winter, the roads and some of the trails are open to snowmobiles. Mountain bikes may be used on the roads and most of the trails. Bikes are not allowed in the West Canada Lakes Wilderness to the south. You might also think about bringing a lightweight canoe to explore some of the ponds.

I served as the state forest ranger in the Moose River Plains for thirty-three years, so I know the region well. The state acquired most of the tract in 1963, when it bought fifty thousand acres from the Gould Paper Company. The Plains (once known as Big Indian Clearing) is an unusual geographical feature in the Adirondacks: a large, gravelly flat with the South Branch of the Moose River, the Red River, and several smaller streams running through it. There also are numerous ponds and lakes. The Plains constitutes the state's second-largest wintering ground for white-tailed deer. As you might guess, the region also attracts moose, which have been making a comeback in the Adirondacks. If you're lucky, you'll see one on the trails or feeding on pond lilies along a shoreline.

The diverse habitats–bogs, boreal forest, upland hardwoods, and mountaintops of spruce–add up to a birder's paradise. Over the years I've seen more than 150 species breeding in the region. In 1971, the last Golden Eagles known to nest in New York State made their home next to the Mitchell Ponds trailhead. The rare Spruce Grouse has nested in the boggy area around Helldiver Pond. Common Loons nest on Squaw, Beaver, Indian, and Little Moose lakes.

The roads, once used for logging, make exploring easy. No matter where you get out of your vehicle, you're sure to hear something singing: Alder Flycatcher in any alder patch, Chestnut-sided Warbler in the brushy areas, White-throated Sparrow at nearly every campsite. All the wood war-

Lost Ponds in the Moose River Plains

blers reside in the Plains. Many of them nest along the roads, including Black-throated Green, Blackburnian, Canada, Yellow-rumped, Magnolia, Northern Parula, and Common Yellowthroat.

Near the bridge over the Red River, you usually can find Mourning Warbler in the blackberry patches. This is also a good spot to observe the courtship flights of the American Woodcock in early June. Scarlet Tanagers can be heard singing near the bridge over Otter Brook on Otter Brook Road. Eastern Phoebes nest under the bridge.

Ring-necked Duck nests on Muskrat Pond and Indian Lake, both located just a tenth of a mile from Indian River Road. They can be observed from the shore of Muskrat, but you'll need a canoe to see them on Indian Lake. In 2007, for the first time, a Canada Goose reared young on Indian Lake.

For those willing to hike into the wilds in search of birds, some suggestions follow.

Lost Ponds. The 0.6-mile trail to Lost Ponds starts at the end of a short spur road on the north side of Moose River Road. For Blackpoll and Bay-breasted Warblers, follow the trail as far as Sumner Stream and then head upstream to an old stillwater, now nearly dry. If you continue on the trail, you should be able to find Gray Jays and Boreal Chickadees around Lost Ponds. Hooded Mergansers often nest on the ponds, while Northern Flickers can be seen on the snags.

Helldiver and Icehouse Ponds. Two short trails, one starting from Moose River Road, the other from Otter Brook Road, lead to these small ponds. On either trail, look for Gray Jays and Boreal Chickadees. Red-eyed Vireos hang out in the deciduous uplands and Blue-headed Vireos near the water. Sometimes a Philadelphia Vireo can be found in the aspens. In early June, the American Woodcock's courtship flights can be seen along the trail to Icehouse Pond. I found nesting Spruce Grouse near Helldiver in the mid-1990s. I haven't seen a Spruce in the area since, but I have seen their scat.

Beaver Lake Trail. A number of interesting species dwell along the 2.3-mile trail to Beaver Lake, which starts at a crossing of Otter Brook. If you have a canoe, you can put in here to paddle a few hundred yards downstream to a stillwater on the Moose, where you can find Indigo Bunting, Alder Flycatcher, Chestnut-sided Warbler, and Common Merganser. The trail passes through some virgin timber. Right at the trailhead you can get Alder Flycatcher, Chestnut-sided Warbler, and Indigo Bunting. Black-backed Woodpeckers have nested in this area, so if you hear tapping or talking trees, look for a nest hole. Ruffed Grouse and Wild Turkey feed their young along this trail. When you reach the lake, look for the resident pair of Common Loons and their chicks. If you brought a canoe, explore the inlet to the southeast and another inlet to the southwest in search of boreal birds such as Yellow-bellied and Olive-sided Flycatchers as well as nesting Eastern Kingbirds. At the west end of the lake you may also find American Bittern, Common and Hooded Mergansers, Mallard, American Black Duck, and Wood Duck. An Osprey nests just down the outlet and fishes along the lakeshore (as do Belted Kingfishers). You should see moose tracks and maybe even a moose along the trail.

Mitchell Ponds. The two-mile trail to Mitchell Ponds from Moose River Road (take the southern branch) runs mostly through a hardwood forest and a limy area that produces some interesting plants. Rattlesnake, maidenhair, and two types of grape fern grow along the trail in a couple of places. You'll also see squirrel corn and Dutchman's-breeches. Wild Turkey and Ruffed Grouse often feed their young along the route. A Least Flycatcher nests and sings every year in a clearing (once the site of a logging camp) just before the first pond. Great Blue Herons fish along the shore of the upper pond, which is reached first. It's also one of the best places to catch otters playing or loons fishing.

White's Pond. The 1.7-mile trail to White's Pond, starting on the north side of Rock Dam Road, crosses through lowland boreal habitat where you can expect to find Black-backed Woodpecker, Gray Jay, and Boreal Chickadee. A variety of other birds inhabits the deciduous habitat. In the early 1970s, the first moose seen in the Adirondacks in decades was spotted at White's Pond. The guy who came across it was so excited that he left his

Moose River Road is the main drag in the Plains.

binoculars behind. I found them the next day hanging from a tree. There were moose tracks all over. In the years since, I and others have seen a number of moose in the vicinity of the pond.

Sly Pond Trail. Starting on the south side of Moose River Road, this trail crosses the South Branch of the Moose and follows a few streams before ending in 5.4 miles at Sly Pond, which lies at three thousand feet. The 3,600-summit of Little Moose Mountain, the highest in the Plains, lies just to the east. The trail gains nearly nine hundred feet, but few people make it all the way to the pond as the last section is overgrown. Besides, most of the good birding comes before the pond, which is virtually dead from acid rain. Rusty Blackbirds nest in the beaver ponds along the route. As you reach the higher elevations near the pond, you get into the territory of the Blackpoll Warbler and Bicknell's Thrush.

Little Moose Lake. Little Moose became property of the state as of January 2007. There are a lot of good birding opportunities along the trail to the lake. It goes over Wilson Ridge. This area was the last to be logged by International Paper, and the changing forest offers very good birding.

Incidentally, the Plains is a great place to watch butterflies, too, with its variety of flowering shrubs and bushes. While on patrol one day, I came across some city fellows looking for Arctic Skippers. I showed them a blackberry patch where I had seen them the day before. They all had butterfly binoculars that focused within a foot of the skippers. I had just gotten a $750 pair of binocs, but I had to stand eight feet away to focus. When I got home, I told my wife that I would be needing new binoculars. She replied that, for $750, I could damn well stand back eight feet. And that's what I'm still doing. **—GL**

Cedar River Flow

Keep an eye out for Common Loon, Osprey, Wilson's Snipe, and a variety of water-fowl, warblers, and boreal birds as you paddle a scenic lake, river, and marsh. Don't miss the heron rookery in the spruce.

DIRECTIONS: From the intersection of NY 28 and NY 30 in Indian Lake, drive 2.2 miles west on NY 28/30 to Cedar River Road on the left (just past the bridge over the river). Turn here and drive 12 miles to a grassy field near the dam that backs up the Cedar River Flow. There is a trail register at the put-in. The road is normally open by Memorial Day weekend, but you may want to wait until after July Fourth—that is, after blackfly season—to do this trip. The flies can be especially pesky here. See map, p.148.

A paddle up the Cedar River Flow and the Cedar River takes you through many birding habitats. Motors are allowed on the flow, but the water is so shallow that they are rare. In five years of watching banded Common Loons here, I saw only four motorboats. The two banded loons nest each year on the flow. It's not unusual to see other loons fishing.

In recent years the flow has been stocked with brown trout. I saw an Osprey pluck out one that was eighteen inches long. I believe Ospreys nest up the river toward Cedar Lakes, because that's where they head with their fish. Bald Eagles also are often seen fishing along the shore. Eagles, Osprey, and Herring Gulls sometimes do battle over a fish.

As you paddle up the flow, look for a Great Blue Heron rookery in the red spruce on the right, where the waterbody narrows to a channel in the reeds. There are a dozen or so nests. Almost always, you'll see adults fishing near the shore. Nesting ducks include Common Mergansers, Mallards,

Photo by Phil Brown

Cedar River Flow

American Black Ducks, and Wood Ducks. In the last few years, Canada Geese have nested and had young.

The area where the channel narrows in the reeds and pond lilies has some of the noisiest birds on the flow. You may hear the winnowing of Wilson's Snipe, the water pump of the American Bittern, and the raucous cuckoo-like calls of the Pied-billed Grebe. If you are patient, you may see these birds with their young. I park myself in the reeds or a pond-lily patch and become part of the flow. Pretty soon peeps of babies trying to get food from mother are heard. If you're lucky, the whole family will come right up to the canoe. If you're really lucky, you may see a moose grazing on the aquatic vegetation.

The upland birds along the flow vary with the habitat. In the mixed hardwoods, you can hear most of the woodland warblers, Winter Wren, Red-eyed and Blue-headed Vireos, Hermit and Swainson's Thrushes, Red-breasted and White-breasted Nuthatches, and Hairy, Downy, Pileated (and sometimes Black-backed) Woodpeckers. In the thicker evergreen forests, Boreal Chickadee, Golden-crowned Kinglet, and Brown Creeper are found.

Ravens and both Red-tailed and Broad-winged Hawks nest along the flow and can be seen gliding across the open areas in search of prey. I've also seen Northern Harriers hunting the marsh at the west end of the flow.

If you venture up the river, you'll find more boreal habitat and many times spot Gray Jay, Black-backed Woodpecker, Boreal Chickadee, Olive-sided Flycatcher, and Yellow-bellied Flycatcher. The Carry Pond lean-to is located about a mile and a half up the river. If you have lunch there, the Gray Jays may join you. On two occasions, both in the second week of July, I've seen great gatherings of swallows in the alders where the river enters the flow. Parents were feeding a hatch of bugs to newly fledged birds. One time there were over a thousand—mostly Tree and Barn Swallows but also some Bank and Northern Rough-winged Swallows. The parents were flying every-where, and the alders were decorated with baby birds.

The Cedar River Flow is about three miles long. Finding the river can be tricky. Look for it on the left shortly after the flow narrows. If you reach the marsh maze at the far end of the flow, you've gone too far (although the marsh is a delight to explore). Beware that when a wind kicks up, the flow can become rough quickly. If that happens, stick to the shore to avoid the waves. **—GL**

Wakely Mountain

Watch for Blackpoll Warbler, Scarlet Tanager, Boreal Chickadee, and Bicknell's Thrush as you climb one of the tallest mountains outside the High Peaks. Try calling for Northern Saw-whet Owl. A fire tower offers a panoramic view.

DIRECTIONS: From the intersection of NY 28 and NY 30 in Indian Lake, drive west on NY 28/30 for 2.2 miles to Cedar River Road. Turn left and go 11.6 miles to the parking lot's entrance on the right. From the west, you also can reach the trailhead by driving through the Moose River Plains Recreation Area to Cedar River Flow and then about a half-mile down Cedar River Road. See **Moose River Plains**.

At 3,744 feet, Wakely Mountain is one of the tallest mountains outside the High Peaks region. A three-mile trail leads to the summit, where a seventy-foot fire tower, the tallest in the state, offers a panoramic view of the central Adirondacks. Along the way you can find some interesting birds. But be warned that there are blackflies along the trail from late May until July, and they can be more than pesky.

The first mile goes through a forest cut in the 1990s by International Paper. The state has since acquired this land. In the new forest growing up, you can hear several warblers, including Black-throated Green, Black-throated Blue, Blackburnian, and Chestnut-sided. Other birds along this stretch are Red-eyed and Blue-headed Vireos, Hermit Thrush, Eastern

Looking out the Wakely Mountain fire tower

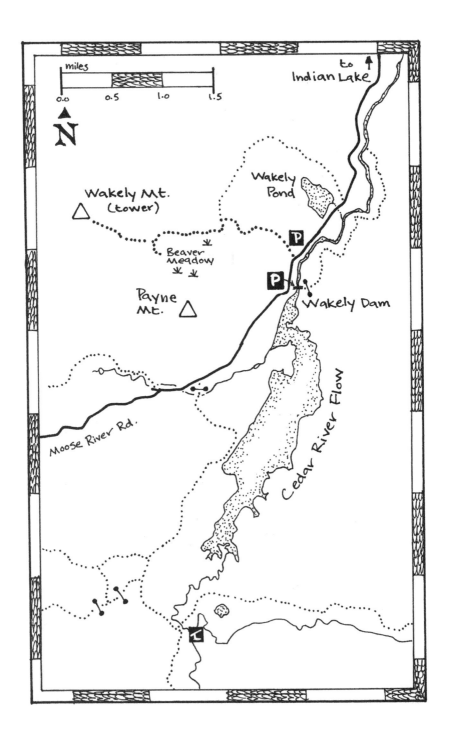

Wood-Pewee, Least Flycatcher, and Rose-breasted Grosbeak.

At 1.9 miles, the foot trail takes a sharp right just before a large beaver pond. The beavers recently flooded the area. It had been a meadow where you could find Northern Waterthrush.

The trail begins climbing after the turn, and it's often steep. As you ascend, the northern hardwood forest changes to white birch, red spruce, and balsam fir. This is where the calls of the woodland warblers, Scarlet Tanager, and Hermit Thrush change to those of Blackpoll Warbler, Boreal Chickadee, and Bicknell's Thrush. These birds are harder to see but nice to listen to as you go to the top. The Boreal Chickadee and Northern Saw-whet Owl sometimes can be called out of the evergreens. A few years ago, I saw two juvenile saw-whets sitting on a branch beside the trail

On the summit, you may hear and see both Blackpoll Warbler and Bicknell's Thrush. Sometimes a crazy American Robin or Barn Swallow will raise its young on the porch of the old observer's cabin. A lonely white elderberry bush between the cabin and the tower gave me my best look at a Bicknell's, which is normally a reclusive bird. I sat on the cabin porch and watched as the bird gorged on the purple-black berries. Climb the tower for a good view of the Moose River Plains, **Cedar River Flow**, and Raquette Lake. Many times while in the tower I have seen Broad-winged Hawks on the hunt gliding below me. **—GL**

The observer cabin on Wakely's summit

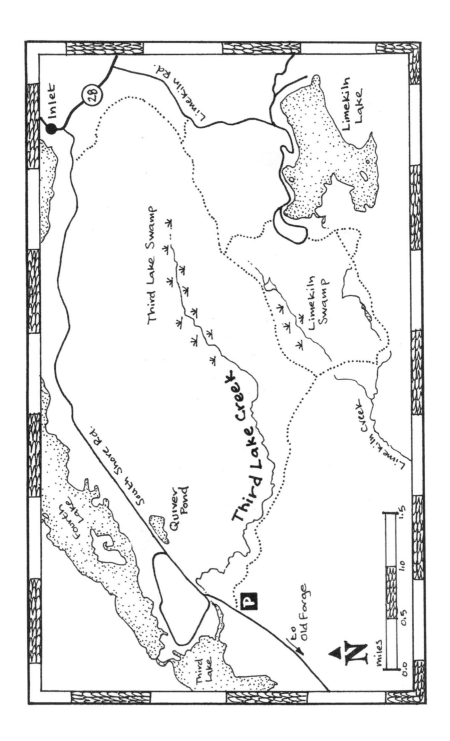

④1 Third Lake Creek

Follow an old logging road through a mature forest that's home to Scarlet Tanager and many kinds of warblers, woodpeckers (including Black-backeds), and boreal birds. You may be able call in a Barred Owl.

DIRECTIONS: The trailhead is on the south side of South Shore Road about halfway between the hamlets of Old Forge and Inlet. From NY 28 in Old Forge, turn south onto South Shore Road and drive about 5 miles to the parking area on the right. If coming from Inlet, turn from NY 28 onto South Shore Road and drive 5.5 miles to the lot, which will be on the left.

The trail is a ski route that goes to the Limekiln Lake State Campground or Limekiln Road, depending which fork you take after a few miles. Birders needn't go that far. Most of the species you'll want to see can be found along the first mile. It's easy walking along an old logging road. Until 1956, Gould Paper Co. dammed the streams in this region for flushing logs to the South Branch of the Moose River.

The first half-mile of the trail goes through a mature forest of mixed hardwoods and red spruce, with lots of small spruce in the understory. Normally you can hear several wood warblers, including Blackburnian, Black-throated Blue, and Black-throated Green, right from the lot. Hairy Woodpecker, Great Crested Flycatcher, and White-breasted Nuthatch nest in the dead stubs around the lot. During the February Backyard Bird Count in 2003, I heard tapping as soon as I got out of the truck: it was a Black-backed Woodpecker working on a tree. Listen for the tapping as you walk down the trail. It could be any of the woodpeckers or a Yellow-bellied Sapsucker.

The trail crosses three pieces of private land, but there is a public right of way. The first private-land signs are those of the Adirondack League Club. This is a good place to see or hear Black-backed Woodpecker and Scarlet Tanager. As you continue, look for Boreal Chickadee in the thick black spruce. The next private parcel was once the homestead of Orley Tuttle,

Photo by Jeff Nadler

Hairy Woodpecker

Start of the Third Lake Creek trail

maker of fishing lures and the Tuttle Bug, a fishing fly made from deer hair. His house sat just off the trail on the left, next to Third Lake Creek and a small feeder stream. Ruffed Grouse and boreal birds hang out near here. If you were to bushwhack along the creek back to South Shore Road, you could find remnants of an old road that led to the homestead, not to mention a variety of birds in the creek's alder swamp and old beaver ponds. I've found Hooded Mergansers and American Black Ducks in pools on the creek.

The trail next passes through mixed softwoods to higher ground, then turns left to pull alongside the creek again, roughly one and a half miles from the road. This is the best spot for Gray Jay and other boreal birds. Many times during the Old Forge Christmas Bird Count I've come here for Gray Jay and called in a Barred Owl. You can hear Common Yellowthroat, Northern Parula, and Nashville Warbler near the opening beside the creek and Golden-crowned Kinglet, Blue-headed Vireo, and Yellow-rumped, Magnolia, and Canada Warblers in the evergreens. The next half-mile of trail is in mixed softwoods, with a few red maples and cherry. Birds to be had include Winter Wren, Dark-eyed Junco, Rose-breasted Grosbeak, Brown Creeper, Red-eyed Vireo, and Blackburnian, Magnolia, Yellow-rumped, and Black-throated Green Warblers. **—GL**

42 South Inlet

Take a leisurely paddle on a peaceful waterway whose bog mat attracts boreal birds. Listen for Wilson's Snipe and American Bittern as well as warblers, flycatchers, and sparrows. Northern Harrier and other hawks hunt here.

DIRECTIONS: From the junction of NY 28 and NY 30 in Blue Mountain Lake, drive west on NY 28 for 10.8 miles to a pull-off on the side of the road, just before the bridge over South Inlet. You'll pass Golden Beach State Campground a little before the pull-off. If you're coming from the west, look for the pull-off 2.6 miles after passing the turn for the hamlet of Raquette Lake. Park on either side of the highway. See map, p. 156.

South Inlet offers a two-mile paddle through boreal habitat to the remnants of an old dam that generated power for Camp Sagamore years ago. The shallow waterway is open to motorboats, but they seldom use it.

Boreal habitat exists on both sides of the inlet for much of its length. It's not uncommon for Gray Jays or Black-backed Woodpeckers to fly from one side to the other. Bog plants grow along the shoreline, including pitcher plants, sundew, cranberries, blue flag, and rose pogonia. If you hear a bird but don't see it, pull over and step onto the sphagnum-moss mat for a closer look. The mat is quite firm, but be careful not to trample it.

Photo by Phil Brown

Relaxing on South Inlet

Photo by Gary Lee

A family of Common Mergansers

In 2007, I paddled South Inlet to conduct a boreal-bird survey for the Wildlife Conservation Society. The whole time I heard American Bitterns calling their *Oong-ka-choonk! Oong-ka-choonk! Oong-ka-choonk!* I flushed two that flew ahead and began calling again. Wilson's Snipe also can be heard along the inlet. Black-backed Woodpeckers had built a nest in a dead stub not far from the shore and were flying back and forth across the water. Olive-sided and Yellow-bellied Flycatchers were singing. I also heard Palm Warbler in a couple of spots—the first time I had encountered this species here. I heard Gray Jays in the first mile but did not see them.

At every stop, I heard the singing of White-throated Sparrows, Swamp Sparrows, and Common Yellowthroats. I was surprised to hear Baltimore Orioles in the poplars near the bridge (I had to see it to believe it) and later Scarlet Tanagers in the evergreens about a half-mile from the road. At a mile and three quarters, I had three singing Lincoln's Sparrows in a large bog mat. Great Crested and Alder Flycatchers sang in a few locations. Wherever the hardwoods came close to the water, I heard wood warblers, including Black-throated Green, Black-throated Blue, Yellow-rumped, Magnolia, Canada, Yellow, Common Yellowthroat, Chestnut-sided, and Northern Waterthrush. Also, Red-eyed and Blue-headed Vireos. Other birds were Pileated and Hairy Woodpeckers, Northern Flicker, Winter Wren, Eastern Bluebird, Northern Parula, Golden-crowned Kinglet, and Red-breasted and White-breasted Nuthatches. Red-tailed and Broad-winged Hawks hunted along the shore. Northern Harriers also hunt and nest in the area. American Black and Wood Ducks, Mallards, and Hooded and Common Mergansers also can be seen on the inlet.

From the dam site, a trail on the left (facing upstream) leads to the Sagamore Loop Trail. Both trails are good for wood warblers. To the right of the dam is a trail that leads to Sagamore Road. This trail is good for warblers and vireos. **—GL**

④③ Raquette Lake Inlets

Escape the big lake on one of these four streams, all rich in birdlife. Among the species you may encounter are Palm Warbler, Lincoln's Sparrow, Yellow-bellied Flycatcher, Boreal Chickadee, Gray Jay, Bald Eagle, and Wood Duck.

DIRECTIONS: From NY 28, turn north on County 2 and follow it 0.4 miles to the parking area in the hamlet of Raquette Lake. You can launch a canoe at the community beach. The turn off NY 28 is next to a power station. If you're coming from the north or east, the turn is 13.4 miles from the junction of NY 28 and NY 30 in the hamlet of Blue Mountain Lake. If you're coming from the south or west, it's about 12 miles from the hamlet of Inlet.

South Inlet is not the only stream flowing into Raquette Lake that is of interest to birders who enjoy paddling. Here are four others, each with good boreal-bird habitat. Some are more navigable than others. You can put in at Raquette Lake hamlet for any of these trips. Beware that the lake gets choppy on windy days. On any of these inlets, you'll probably have the place to yourself. Bring a lunch and a pair of binoculars, and enjoy.

Marion River. From the hamlet paddle north along the west side of Big Island, round Long Point, and head east up the bay to the mouth of the Marion River. Once on the river, you'll have about two miles of flatwater. Most of the boreal habitat is on the south side. Not many of the boreal species fly across the river, but they can be seen and heard in their habitat. When I did this trip in 2007, I had Black-backed Woodpecker, Olive-sided and Yellow-bellied Flycatchers, and Lincoln's Sparrow. Gray Jays and Boreal Chickadees also live along the river, though I didn't get any that day. I also saw two Bald Eagles, one adult and one immature, and Great Blue Herons. Lots of wood warblers were singing along the shore. At the end of the flatwater, it's possible to portage to Utowana Lake and continue paddling to Eagle Lake and Blue Mountain Lake.

Boulder Brook. The most difficult of the four inlets to canoe is Boulder Brook, the outlet of the Sargent Ponds. To reach it, paddle north from the hamlet past Long Point and Osprey Island and then round Tioga Point to enter Boulder Bay (a state campground is on the south side of the bay). The brook is at the bay's northeast corner. You need to go over only the first three beaver dams to see the best bird habitat. When you get to a log fallen across the entire width of the brook, it's a good time to turn around. When I did this trip, I saw a mature Bald Eagle perched in a tree at the mouth, watching a family of Common Mergansers. Other birds logged that day were Black-backed Woodpecker, Olive-sided and Yellow-bellied Flycatchers, Wood Duck, American Black Duck, Swamp and Song

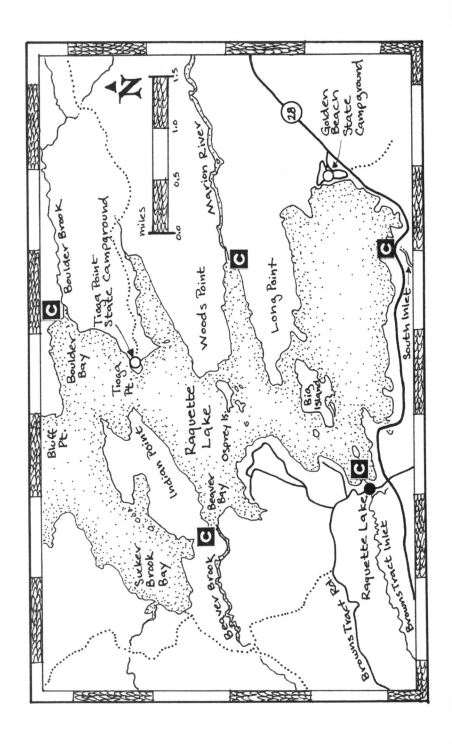

Exploring Browns Tract Inlet

Sparrows, Common Yellowthroat, Northern Parula, Chestnut-sided Warbler, Alder Flycatcher, and Winter Wren. Farther up the brook, I saw Red-tailed and Broad-winged Hawks.

Browns Tract Inlet. This twisting stream, decorated with pond lilies and pickerelweed, is on the Adirondack Canoe Route, which goes from Old Forge to Saranac Lake. The inlet enters Raquette Lake in the bay south of the hamlet. Once you get over the first beaver dam, you'll have nearly two miles of clear paddling to the portage trail on the south shore. This stretch covers most of the boreal-bird habitat. Pitcher plants, sundews, and wild roses grow along the banks. Since this habitat lies on both sides, boreal birds often fly across the stream. When I did the trip in 2007, I saw Black-backed Woodpecker, Gray Jay, Lincoln's Sparrow, and Olive-sided and Yellow-bellied Flycatchers, all along the water. Several American Bittern and Wilson's Snipe were heard. Wood warblers and vireos could also be heard singing where the hardwoods come close to the water. At the portage trail there is a five-hundred-foot raised boardwalk. It's a great spot for Northern Waterthrush and an excellent platform for observing boreal birds, with a bog on one side and an alder swamp on the other. I saw a Marsh Wren here in late summer in 2007–the only one I've seen in the Adirondacks. Years ago, a Sora with babies went under the boardwalk while I was standing on it. After I got in my canoe, she brought them right to the water's edge.

Beaver Brook. This is another stream with boggy boreal habitat on both sides. Paddle north from the hamlet, round Antler Point, and head northwest across Beaver Bay. The brook enters the lake at the bay's northern cove. Once on the brook, you'll have to go over a beaver dam not far from the lake and another one farther upstream, but Beaver Brook is well worth the effort. The rose pogonias were in bloom when I paddled the brook in mid-July in 2007. As for birds, I had a family of Gray Jays, Black-backed Woodpecker, Palm Warbler, Olive-sided and Yellow-bellied Flycatchers, and Lincoln's, Swamp, and Song Sparrows. I also saw two families of Wood Ducks and one family of Mallards. When you reach the alder bed, after a mile and a half, it's time to turn around. **—GL**

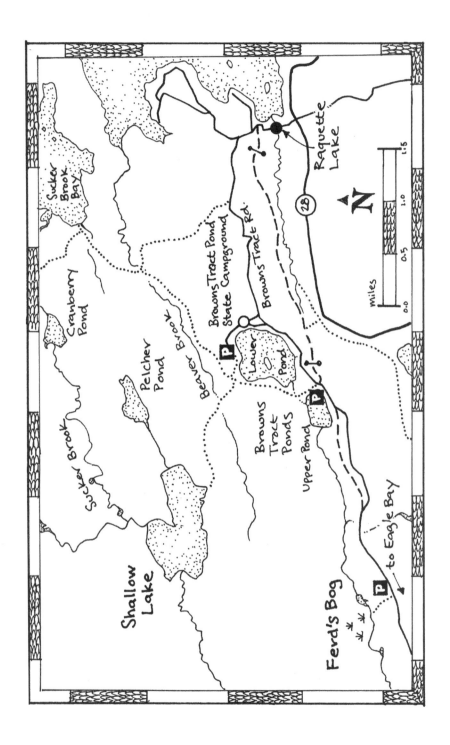

 **Shallow Lake**

On the trail to the lake, stop at a bog to listen for American Three-toed Woodpecker, Nashville Warbler, Lincoln's Sparrow, Palm Warbler, and Olive-sided Flycatcher. Common Loon, Osprey, and Bald Eagle fish in the lake.

DIRECTIONS: You can hike to Shallow Lake from Uncas Road (also known as Browns Tract Road) or from Browns Tract Ponds State Campground, whose entrance is on the same road. Starting from the campground shortens the hike by 0.7 miles, but a day-use fee is required. From NY 28 between Blue Mountain Lake and Inlet, turn north on County 2, drive 0.7 miles through the hamlet of Raquette Lake to Uncas Road, then turn left. The campground is 1.9 miles up the road. The other trailhead is reached after 2.9 miles, next to Upper Browns Tract Pond.

If you start from Uncas Road, take the Sucker Brook Bay Trail 0.9 miles to the Shallow Lake Trail on the left. If you start from the campground, take the 0.2-mile connector trail (near Campsite 68) to the Sucker Brook Bay Trail, then turn left, and you'll shortly reach the Shallow Lake Trail on the right. From the junction, it's 1.6 miles to Shallow Lake.

The Shallow Lake Trail crosses a bog through which Beaver Brook flows. When we built the three-log bridge over the brook, we saw all the boreal birds, and Gray Jays had lunch with us both days. It's a good spot to look for boreal species. I once observed, just before the brook, a Spruce Grouse with young feeding on blueberries along the trail. I saw Spruce Grouse scat here in 2008. After crossing the brook, at 0.6 miles, you'll see a bog mat where southern twayblades, white fringed orchis, and rose pogonias grow. If you leave the trail and go downstream a bit, you'll come to a place where the bog mat completely covers Beaver Brook. It's larger than the mat at Ferd's Bog. I have found Palm Warblers nesting here in recent years. Nashville Warblers always can be heard singing in June and early July, but they are hard to locate. They nest in the sphagnum moss but sing high up in the trees around the bog. Both Black-backed and American Three-toed Woodpeckers can be attracted by making a few Barred Owl calls. The best way to locate them is to listen for their *twek* calls and their tapping. Numerous Lincoln's, Swamp, and White-throated Sparrows nest under the small black spruce trees on the bog mat. I usually have found several Yellow-bellied and a few Olive-sided Flycatchers as well.

Returning to the trail, you'll remain in boreal habitat most of the way to Shallow Lake, though you will pass through a stand of large, open hardwoods where Scarlet Tanager can be heard. Brown Creepers nest under the curled bark of yellow birch along this stretch of trail, though they feed mostly on the rough bark of hemlocks. Most of the wood warblers also can be seen and heard.

The bog on the way to Shallow Lake

As you get close to the lake, look for a hidden canoe, as there is usually one around. If you carry in a paddle and life vest, you'll be able to explore the lake and the boggy inlet at the west end. Once you reach the water, walk left to a small point that offers a view of the entire lake. There is a resident pair of Common Loons. Herring Gulls also can be found. When I first visited Shallow Lake, in 1966, there was an Osprey nest in a pine near the outlet. At that time, there was only one other Osprey nest anywhere near here, on Squaw Lake in the Moose River Plains. In recent years, Ospreys have nested just over a hill, but they fish on Shallow, which has a good population of smallmouth bass and sunfish. Bald Eagles fish here, too. Many times I've visited Shallow after the first snows, just before the lake freezes, and seen big flocks of ducks gathered for the journey south: Common and Hooded Mergansers, Bufflehead, Common Goldeneye, Mallard, and American Black.

When you get back to Uncas Road at the Upper Pond, you'll notice a dirt road just across from the trailhead. This takes you to the old railroad bed that goes to Raquette Lake. If you follow it a short distance, you'll come to a nice bog where most of the boreal birds can be found. A fellow from New York City came up to Ferd's Bog in search of the boreal species. He camped there more than once but could never find the birds he wanted. So I suggested he try the railroad bed. He camped in an old borrow pit just down the trail, and in two days he got all the boreal birds except Spruce Grouse, right from his campsite.

Another idea is to take the Sucker Brook Bay Trail all the way to Sucker Brook Bay on Raquette Lake. The bay is 2.2 miles from the Shallow Lake turnoff. The woods along this stretch of trail were hit hard by a 1995 windstorm, creating good bird habitat. Look for Black-backed Woodpecker, Gray Jay, and wood warblers. **—GL**

45 Ferd's Bog

Be sure to visit this place, one of Adirondack birders' favorite sites for boreal species, including American Three-toed and Black-backed Woodpeckers. On the short trail to the bog mat, you'll also have a chance to see Brown Creeper, Winter Wren, vireos, and several types of warblers.

DIRECTIONS: From NY 28 in the hamlet of Eagle Bay, turn north onto Uncas Road and drive 3.5 miles to a small parking area on the left. See map, p. 158.

Ferd's Bog is famed among birders as a place to find boreal species. In the late 1990s, a plastic-lumber boardwalk was built to keep visitors from trampling the sensitive bog (actually, it's a fen, which is fed by groundwater). The hike from the road to the boardwalk is only three-tenths of a mile. The trail descends through hardwoods and mixed woods to a spruce-fir flat. On the way down, if it's the right season, listen for the singing of warblers: Blackburnian, Black-throated Blue, Black-throated Green, and Ovenbird. Also along the trail are Winter Wren, Dark-eyed Junco, Brown Creeper, White-breasted Nuthatch, Yellow-bellied Sapsucker, Hermit Thrush, Red-eyed and Blue-headed Vireos, and Hairy and Pileated Woodpeckers. Once you get to the evergreens, you should hear Golden-crowned Kinglet and Nashville, Palm, Yellow-rumped, and Magnolia Warblers. Also be alert for Red-breasted Nuthatch, Boreal Chickadee, Gray Jay, Yellow-bellied and Olive-sided Flycatchers, and the tapping of Black-backed and American Three-toed Woodpeckers, all of which nest here.

The first 150 feet of the boardwalk pass through the black spruce and tamarack that skirt the bog mat. This is a good location to watch for boreal birds as they circulate around the bog feeding. It's also a pretty spot. The green carpet of sphagnum moss covers every hump and bump on the forest floor. Creeping snowberry, a small round-leaf plant that grows over the moss, produces in July a white berry that's flavored like mint. Southern twayblade, an orchid at its most northern fringe, grows along the side of the boardwalk. In the open bog are sundews, pitcher plants, white fringed orchis, grass-pinks, and several types of sedges. Listen now for Lincoln's, White-throated, and Swamp Sparrows, Common Yellowthroat, Tree Swallow, and Eastern Bluebird. Many of the boreal birds fly across the bog and may be attracted by giving a few Barred Owl hoots.

One day I walked down to the bog in peak blackfly season and met two men sitting in lawn chairs at the end of the boardwalk. They both wore head nets, but they had been bitten more than once. When I asked if they had seen anything, they said a Boreal Chickadee was feeding young to the left of

Birders at Ferd's Bog

the boardwalk. They said they were looking for the Black-backed Woodpecker. I made a few owl calls, and a Black-backed gave a couple of *kiks* and landed right on a tree stub not fifteen feet from us. "Is that all you do?" one of the men asked. "We have been here for two days waiting for it to show up."

Ferd's Bog is named after Ferdinand LaFrance, an avid birder from the Syracuse area who had a camp on Uncas Road. He used to go through the bog to hunt deer on Cascade Ridge. He saw all the boreal birds and soon began leading trips here for the Onondaga Audubon Society. After his article "Ferd's Bog" appeared in the *The Kingbird* in October 1975, the name stuck.

Ferd and I had talked a few times over the phone in 1980. At that time, both of us were working on *The Atlas of Breeding Birds in New York State*. We never met until late one night in July 1981. Ferd called me from the porch of Higby Lodge on Big Moose Lake and said they wouldn't let him inside because he looked so awful. He and Chris Spies had been birding for the atlas, working their way from Shallow Lake west toward Queer Lake through bogs and black spruce in the pouring rain. They came out in the dark. He asked if I would give them a ride back to camp. And so twenty minutes later I met Ferdinand Lafrance. His pants were torn right to his crotch, and he looked like he had been dragged through mud. After that, we became fast friends, often birding together. Ferd's hearing had failed, so I was his ears, but when he got his binoculars on a bird, it was instant identification. Ferd died in 1997. —**GL**

46 Woodhull Lake

Look for waterbirds while touring the lake in a canoe or kayak. Five pairs of Common Loon nest here. Other species observed include Double-crested Cormorant, Red-throated Loon, Ring-necked Duck, Wood Duck, Bald Eagle, and Merlin.

DIRECTIONS: From NY 28, just south of the bridge over the Moose River, turn east onto McKeever Road. Go 0.3 miles to a junction, continuing straight on a dirt road that goes past the former train station. After crossing the tracks you'll come to a large parking lot with a trail register. After signing in, drive through the lot to a gravel road and take this 4.7 miles to its end. From there, it's 500 feet to a put-in on Woodhull Lake.

Woodhull Lake became more accessible a few years ago with the construction of a gravel road that leads almost to its shore. You can stop to bird on the way to the lake, but be careful not to block the one-lane road. There are some campsites and a few other places where you can pull off. There is little traffic as not many people know about the access road—yet.

Near the trail register and the railroad tracks, you can find Yellow and Chestnut-sided Warblers and Indigo Bunting in the second-growth hardwoods. On the way to the lake, the road passes through hardwood forest where most of the wood warblers can be heard and seen. Ruffed Grouse and their young often feed along the road. You also can see Red-tailed and Broad-winged Hawks perching and hunting for mice and chipmunks. Sometimes they fly ahead and land again to give you another look at them. Scarlet Tanager, Rose-breasted Grosbeak, Least Flycatcher, Winter Wren, and Dark-eyed Junco also can be found along the corridor.

Woodhull Lake is shaped like a boomerang. The state owns most of the west arm and maintains a few marked campsites. The rest of the lake is

Woodhull Lake

Photo by Phil Brown

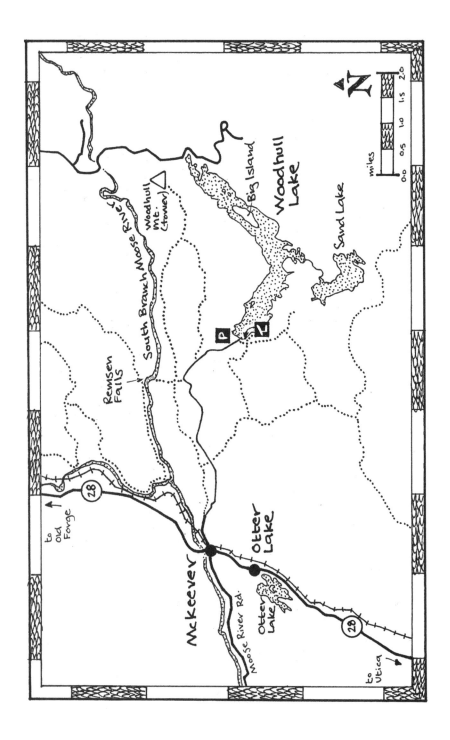

owned and posted by the Adirondack League Club and fifteen or so private camps (more development is in the offing). You may paddle anywhere on the lake, but don't get out on private land. Five pairs of Common Loons nest here, producing some chicks each year. Some of the loons build their nests on man-made wooden rafts, so look for these if you're paddling before mid-July. A pair of Great Blue Herons nests on the small island in the northwest part of the lake (that's why the island is closed to camping). Loons sometimes nest there as well. As of 2007, only one pair of Herring Gulls was nesting on the lake; there had been three pairs a few years earlier. Other waterbirds I've seen include Double-crested Cormorant, Red-throated Loon, Ring-necked Duck, Wood Duck, American Black Duck, Mallard, and both Hooded and Common Mergansers. Look for Spotted Sandpiper along the shoreline. Broad-winged Hawks have nested on Big Island (privately owned) for years and often can be seen carrying food to their young. A new arrival is the Merlin, which has nested on the north shore in recent years. These falcons make a lot of noise when they have young out and about. A Bald Eagle has been visiting the lake, preying on baby ducks and loons. When it's around, the loons will be hollering.

Most of the wood warblers can be heard if you paddle near the shore. Woodhull has the largest concentration of Black-and-white and Blackburnian Warblers of all the lakes I visit. Hairy and Downy Woodpeckers, Yellow-bellied Sapsucker, Chimney Swift, Tree and Barn Swallows, and Least and Great Crested Flycatchers can be heard as well. Beware that this lake gets rough with a west wind, and you'll be heading into it on the way back to the put-in.   **—GL**

Tree Swallow

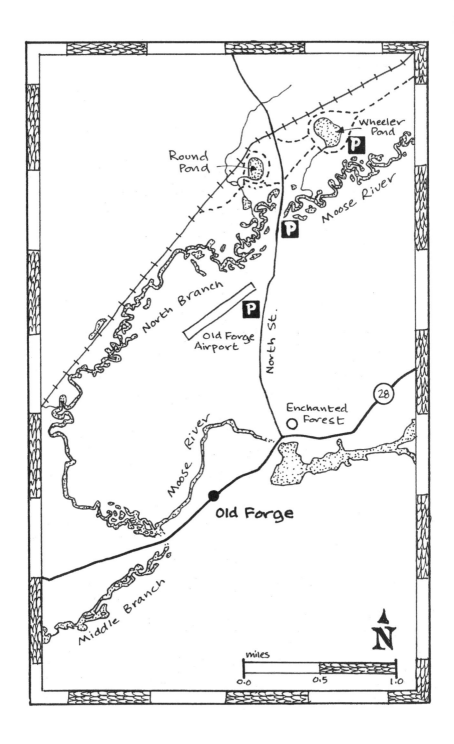

47 Wheeler Pond Loop

Explore from the car the wetlands and woods along the North Branch of the Moose River. You usually can find lots of warblers as well as northern species such as Boreal Chickadee, Gray Jay, and Black-backed Woodpecker.

DIRECTIONS: From NY 28 in the hamlet of Old Forge, turn north on North Street. This road turns to dirt after a while and crosses the North Branch of the Moose River, leading to a network of wide trails used by snowmobilers in winter and mountain bikers in other seasons. Most of these routes usually can be driven from early June (after mud season) until Sept. 1, when they are used by hunting clubs that lease the land.

The dirt roads to and around Wheeler Pond offer plenty of good birding, but you should start looking for birds well before you reach the pond. As you drive up North Street, keep an eye out for an abandoned gravel pit on the right, just past the soccer field. You'll find lots of butterflies, because it's full of milkweed. Indigo Bunting have nested near the clearing for several years, and you may hear them singing in the taller trees. Just up the road on the left, another gravel pit has the largest Bank Swallow colony in the Old Forge region. You also can find some neat birds, including Wilson's Snipe, Eastern Bluebird, and Indigo Bunting, at the former Old Forge Airport, which is kept mowed for model-plane fans. Listen for the winnowing of snipe along the North Branch of the Moose River.

Soon after the road turns to dirt, you'll cross the river. On the other side is a flat area covered by a tangle of alder and red osier, a great place for birds. Nesting here are Gray Catbird, Brown Thrasher, Alder Flycatcher, Yellow and Chestnut-sided Warblers, Common Yellowthroat, Cedar Waxwing, Wilson's Snipe, Belted Kingfisher, and American Bittern. Cardinal flowers and turtleheads bloom along here in early August.

A little past the flat, turn right off the main road for the two-mile Wheeler Pond Loop. Wheeler Pond itself doesn't offer much to birders, but the forest along the route (which has been logged) has a variety of habitat. As many as five pairs of Mourning Warblers have nested in the blackberry patches on the loop. These birds are hard to spot but have a distinctive call, a low, loud *check*. Other woodland warblers on the loop include Black-throated Blue, Black-throated Green, Magnolia, Yellow-rumped, and Blackburnian. Also look for Blue-headed and Red-eyed Vireos. Barred Owl calls may produce a response or even drum up a Broad-winged Hawk or Northern Goshawk. These calls also will beckon Hairy, Downy, and Pileated Woodpeckers and Northern Flickers. But perhaps the most curious bird, one that almost always comes to this call, is the Yellow-bellied Sapsucker. If you see the sapsucker's holes on a tree, you shouldn't have to wait long to see a Ruby-throated Hummingbird checking them for bugs. Hermit Thrush, Winter Wren, White-breasted Nuthatch, and Brown Creeper can be heard all along the loop.

About halfway around, just before making a sharp left toward the west, you come closest to the boreal bog habitat along the river (on your right). If you take a short walk south off the road, you should hear Gray Jay, Boreal Chickadee, Black-backed Woodpecker, Yellow-bellied and Olive-sided Flycatchers, Sharp-shinned Hawk, Red-breasted Nuthatch, Magnolia, Canada, and Nashville Warblers, Northern Waterthrush, Golden-crowned Kinglet, and Lincoln's, Swamp, and White-throated Sparrows.

Before completing the loop in your car, you'll pass another road leading east to more bog habitat. It's an opportunity to observe boreal birds right from the road. When I was birding with Dorothy Crumb here a few years ago, we came across Baltimore checkerspot butterflies feeding on flowers next to the road. It's the only place I've seen the butterflies up here. **—GL**

Many birds frequent the alders along the North Branch.

Photo by Phil Brown

Common Loon

Plate 9

Spruce Grouse

Olive-sided Flycatcher

Yellow-bellied Flycatcher

Plate 10

Osprey

Merlin

Bald Eagle

Plate 11

Gray Jay

Plate 12

Bicknell's Thrush

Plate 13

Tennessee Warbler

Bay-breasted Warbler

Cape May Warbler

Yellow Palm Warbler

Plate 14

Rusty Blackbird

White-throated Sparrow

Lincoln's Sparrow

Ruby-crowned Kinglet

Plate 15

Evening Grosbeak

American Three-toed Woodpecker

White-winged Crossbill

Plate 16

48 Big Moose Lake

Paddle across the lake to a quiet inlet inhabited by Common and Hooded Mergansers, Mallards, and Wood Duck. Common Loon and Merlin also nest on the lake. For boreal species, hike from the lake to one of the interior ponds.

DIRECTIONS: From the hamlet of Eagle Bay on NY 28, drive north on Big Moose Road for 4.0 miles to Higby Road on the right. Paddlers should turn here and drive to a public dock at the end of the road. Motorboats can be launched at Dunn's Boat Livery, a little farther up Big Moose Road beyond the Higby turn. Those hiking to Constable Pond can park on Higby Road near the start of Judson Road and walk down Judson to the trail proper.

Big Moose Lake is a 1,265-acre waterbody with several fingers: East Bay, South Bay, North Bay, and, at the easternmost end, the Inlet, which has an extensive marsh. The lake gets rough with a west wind, though paddlers can seek shelter in North Bay or the Inlet. In July and August, the lake sees a lot of motorboat traffic. There is good birding both on the lake and along nearby trails.

On the lake, look for warblers along the shoreline. Many ducks nest in the Inlet, including Mallards, Common and Hooded Mergansers, and sometimes Wood Ducks. The lake boasts three pairs of nesting Common Loons, one on each of the main bays. In recent years, Merlins have nested in North Bay. Broad-winged Hawks usually can be seen hunting around the lake. Two Osprey that nest on nearby Mays Pond often fish in the lake—a sign that Big Moose is recovering from acid rain. Once nearly devoid of fish,

Hooded Merganser

the lake now has largemouth bass, perch, bullhead, and some lake trout and brook trout. Accordingly, some of the fish-eating birds have returned. You may even see a Bald Eagle soaring overhead, although no nesting has been documented.

Three foot trails accessible only by water lead to good birding sites. The first leads from the north side of the Inlet to Gull Lakes and a lean-to

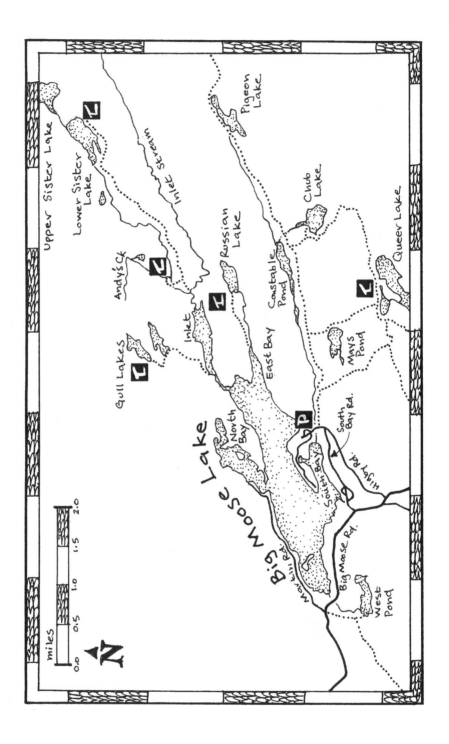

The Inlet on Big Moose Lake

Photo by Phil Brown

(reached after 1.2 miles). This area was hit hard by a 1995 windstorm, resulting in a lot of new growth and a changing bird habitat. From the end of the Inlet another trail leads 3.3 miles to a lean-to on Lower Sister Lake (with the option of a half-mile side trip to the Andy's Creek lean-to). The third starts at East Bay and goes 0.8 miles to the lean-to at Russian Lake. A fourth trail leads from Judson Road, just south of the lake, to Constable Pond, Queer Lake, and other ponds in the 50,100-acre Pigeon Lake Wilderness.

All the trails go through good boreal-bird habitat. Nesting loons can be found on many of the interior ponds. There is a small rookery of Great Blue Herons on Constable Pond. On most of the hikes you'll hear a lot of wood warblers singing, and Gray Jays may greet you on any of the trails or near the lean-tos. On a trip to the Lower Sister Lake lean-to in the fall of 2006, I saw Boreal Chickadee, Gray Jay, and Black-backed Woodpecker. The fall colors were in full riot, but I saw some lingering warblers, both Red-breasted and White-breasted Nuthatches, and Golden-crowned Kinglets. The loons were still feeding a big chick on the lake. Take one of these side trips and get away from it all; stay overnight in a lean-to and listen to dueling Barred Owls searching for food. Northern Saw-whets Owls also nest in the region, so you may hear their toots, even during the day. **—GL**

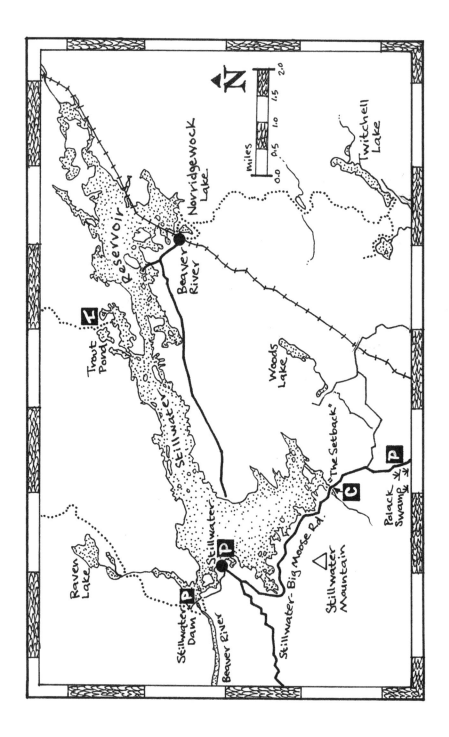

Reservoir

Norridgewock
Lake

Beaver
River

Trout
Pond

Twitchell
Lake

Woods
Lake

"The Setback"

Stillwater

Black
Swamp

Stillwater

Stillwater–Big Moose Rd.

Stillwater
Mountain

Raven
Lake

Stillwater
Dam

Beaver River

N

miles

0.0 0.5 1.0 1.5 2.0

Stillwater Reservoir

If you love loons, you'll want to paddle this remote waterbody, which boasts sixteen nesting pairs. Merlins, ducks, and lots of warblers also dwell here. On the drive in, stop at a roadside swamp to check for boreal species.

DIRECTIONS: From NY 28 in Eagle Bay, drive north and west on Big Moose Road and Stillwater Road. After 18 miles, turn right onto the access road for the boat launch on Stillwater Reservoir. (You can also reach the launch from Lowville in the west via the Number Four Road and Stillwater Road.) Alternatively, you can put in a canoe at the southwest corner of the reservoir, where the Stillwater Road crosses the water. This spot, known as the Setback, is 14.4 miles from Eagle Bay.

At 6,034 acres, Stillwater Reservoir is the fourth-largest waterbody within the Adirondack Park (not including Lake Champlain). At the state boat launch, there are bathrooms, a large parking area, and a registration booth for campers. The forty-six campsites around the resevoir are free, available on a first-come, first-served basis. Paddlers should be aware that the reservoir gets rough on windy days. If you're running an outboard, you need to steer clear of the many rock shoals and stumps.

The reservoir has sixteen pairs of nesting Common Loons, the largest loon population in the state. It can be tough for the loons if the water level fluctuates a lot. In wet years, their nests get flooded; in dry years, when water may be drawn down three to six feet, the birds sometimes have trouble getting back on their nests. Nevertheless, some of them usually manage to fledge chicks, according to biologist Judy McIntyre, who has monitored the loons for more than twenty-five years.

The boat launch at Stillwater Reservoir

Photo by Phil Brown

Photo by Gary Lee

A Common Loon taking a shower

Bald Eagles have been hanging around Stillwater in recent years, but no nest has been found. The eagles harass and catch loon chicks as well as the chicks of Mallards and Common Mergansers. Merlins nest along the shoreline, mostly in tall pines. You can hear them especially when their young are first fledged and begging for food.

The reservoir has many bays and fingers, some of which had been lakes themselves before the dam was built. While paddling in these quiet corners, you can see and hear many wood warblers. Tree and Barn Swallows are always catching bugs over the water. One pair of Barn Swallows built a nest on the party barge that goes back and forth from the boat launch to the tiny community of Beaver River. The swallows followed the boat, feeding their young as it went.

The reservoir's many sandbars attract birds during fall migration, such as Whimbrels and various sandpipers. You never know what you're going to encounter around the next bend.

About two miles before the Setback (4.3 miles from the old Big Moose station), you'll pass Polack Swamp on the left, just past a big gravel pit on the right. The land is all private, but it's worth stopping to observe birds from the road. In 2007, a Black-backed Woodpecker occupied a nest hole 150 feet from the culvert. I've seen American Three-toed Woodpecker with young, Boreal Chickadee, and Gray Jay. A few years back, I saw a Cooper's Hawk chasing a Northern Flicker among the dead stubs. Lincoln's, Swamp, and Song Sparrows, Common Yellowthroat, Magnolia and Yellow-rumped Warblers, and Eastern Bluebirds have all nested here. **—GL**

50 Pepperbox Wilderness

Bushwhack into a rarely visited Wilderness Area in search of boreal birds or walk a dirt road, closed to vehicles, at the Wilderness boundary. Birds seen along the road include Eastern Phoebe, Broad-winged Hawk, and Black-throated Blue Warbler.

DIRECTIONS: From NY 28 in Eagle Bay, drive about 18 miles on the Big Moose and Stillwater roads (the latter is dirt) to a T intersection. Turn right onto the paved access road for **Stillwater Reservoir**. Go 0.5 miles and turn left onto a dirt road just before the parking lot for the reservoir's boat launch. The road goes past the Stillwater dam, ending after a mile at a gated bridge over the Beaver River. (This is where canoeists put in the Moshier Reservoir.) If you're coming from Lowville in the west, the Stillwater Reservoir is reached via the Number Four and Stillwater roads.

The 22,560-acre Pepperbox Wilderness lacks marked hiking trails. However, after crossing a bridge over the Beaver River you can continue walking on a jeep road that forms its southeastern boundary. The road allows landowners access to a small inholding on Raven Lake. A good destination is Shallow Pond, located about two miles from the bridge. The pond is connected to Raven Lake. Beyond this point, the trail continues into the **Five Ponds Wilderness**.

Most of my birding forays have been along the Raven Lake road. Eastern Phoebes nest under the bridge, and for several years Broad-winged Hawks nested not far up the road. Black-throated Blue and Black-throated Green Warblers and Common Yellowthroats can be seen as well.

Bridge at the start of the Raven Lake trail

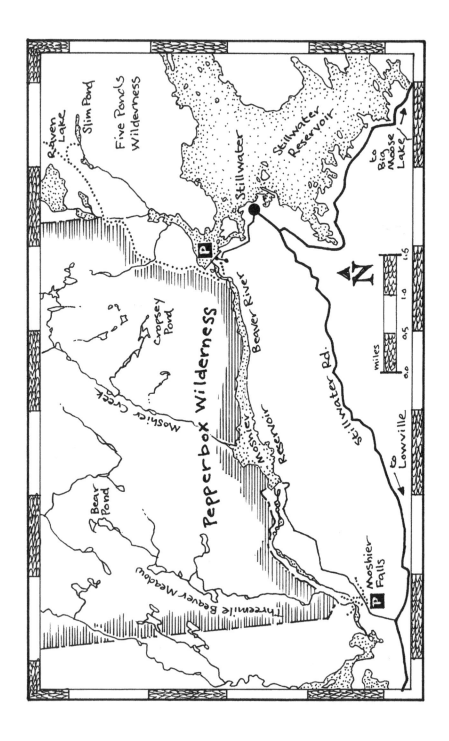

Another option is to walk along the north shore of Moshier Reservoir. Hiking along the reservoir, you can hear Scarlet Tanager, Rose-breasted Grosbeak, Least Flycatcher, White-throated Sparrow, Swamp Sparrow, and many of the warblers. I've watched the Common Loons on the reservoir for years, and most of the time I have the place to myself. Most of the bigger interior waterbodies in this Wilderness Area—including Pepperbox, Sunshine, Deer, and Moshier ponds—have had nesting loons even though some of them contained no fish.

The Pepperbox also can be accessed via a short access trail at the

Sign at Moshier Reservoir

Moshier Reservoir dam. Much of the region is hardwoods, but get near a pond or brook and you'll find plenty of softwood timber. In my explorations, I've come across many old beaver ponds with lots of good birds, such as Ring-necked Duck and Hooded Merganser. I've also seen several Olive-sided and Yellow-bellied Flycatchers around these old beaver ponds, plus lots of Least Flycatchers.

The Pepperbox certainly has good habitat for boreal birds, but I haven't seen as many of these as you'd expect. Maybe I just missed them while swatting flies. I did have a few Black-backed Woodpeckers, Gray Jays, and Boreal Chickadees. Other species I've logged here include Bald Eagles, Merlins, and Cooper's Hawks.

I never saw another person on any of my travels, though I did find evidence of campsites at some ponds. For those with the requisite outdoors skills, the Pepperbox is one of the more adventuresome places to bird in the Adirondacks. If you do any bushwhacking, be sure to bring a map and compass. **—GL**

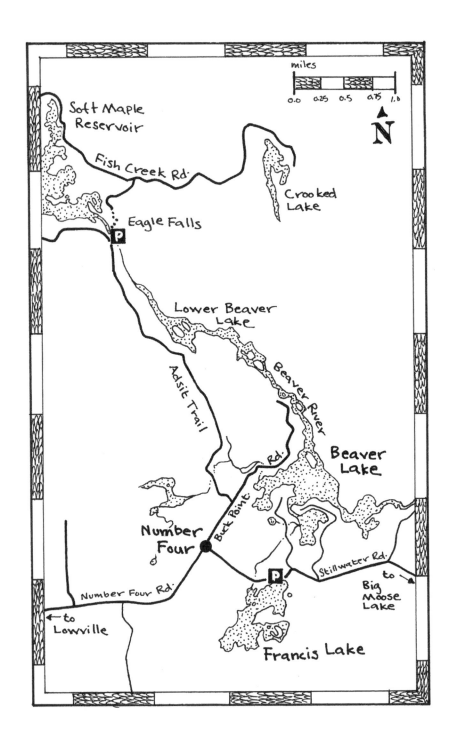

51 Beaver Lake

Paddle up the lake to observe a wide diversity of birds, including Scarlet Tanager, Northern Parula, Belted Kingfisher, Song Sparrow, Alder Flycatcher, Black-backed Woodpecker, Eastern Wood-Pewee, Wood Duck, and Merlin.

DIRECTIONS: From NY 28 in Eagle Bay, drive north and west on Big Moose Road and Stillwater Road. After 18 miles, turn left at the stop sign near Stillwater and drive 7.9 miles to an intersection with Number Four Road. Turn right onto Buck Point Road. After about a half-mile, turn left on Adsit Trail, a dirt road. Follow this for 2.6 miles, turn right at a canoe-carry sign, and drive to a parking area near the Eagle Falls dam. Much of the driving will be on dirt roads. You can also reach the put-in by driving east out of Lowville on Number Four Road. Buck Point Road is about 18 miles from Lowville.

Beaver Lake has two parts. Lower Beaver Lake is long and narrow like a river. Upper Beaver Lake is more like a regular lake. Upper Beaver has no direct public access, but you can put in a canoe at the Eagle Falls dam at the outlet of Lower Beaver and paddle to the upper lake. Be sure to put in above the rope at the dam. If water is being released from the dam, there will be some current between the lakes. The land along both waterbodies is privately owned.

At the put-in, I have seen both Spotted Sandpiper and Blue-headed Vireo with young and Black-throated Green Warbler carrying food to a nest. Not far from the dam, you'll hear Scarlet Tanagers singing just about every year in late spring and early summer. You can see many warblers along the Lower Beaver, including Northern Parula, Black-throated Blue, Blackburnian, Nashville, Magnolia, Yellow-rumped, and Northern Waterthrush. Belted Kingfishers often fish along the shore. In recent years, one pair of Common Loons has nested on Lower Beaver, while two pairs have nested on Upper Beaver.

As I was going up the lower lake a few years ago, I heard a Black-backed Woodpecker. It flew overhead and landed on the larger of the two islands.

Lower Beaver Lake

Photo by Phil Brown

The woodpecker was carrying food, so I looked for the nest hole, but darkness came before I could find it. I returned the next day to take photos of newly hatched loons. While paddling through the narrowest part of the lake, I heard a talking tree: a pair of juvenile Black-backeds begging for food. Both parents came and fed the young while I snapped pictures. Although Beaver Lake is outside this boreal woodpecker's territory, the shoreline resembles its bog habitat farther north. This was the first time I found Black-backeds nesting in a hardwood tree.

Great Blue Herons often feed in the shallows. Each little bay of the lower lake has Common Grackles, Red-winged Blackbirds, and White-throated, Song, and Swamp Sparrows nesting.

Many times I've seen otters and mink playing along the shoreline of Lower Beaver. There is only one camp along the lower lake, and it's partially hidden by the trees.

Nearing Upper Beaver, you'll pass through some quick water and under an old footbridge to enter a narrow channel that harbors Alder Flycatcher, Purple Finch, American Goldfinch, Yellow Warbler, Chestnut-sided Warbler, Pine Warbler, Yellow-bellied Sapsucker, and Hairy and Downy Woodpeckers. This lake has three children's camps, where I've heard the singing of Least Flycatchers, Eastern Phoebes, and Eastern Wood-Pewees. In July and August, you should expect to see other canoes, kayaks, sailboats, and perhaps a few powerboats on the upper lake. Most don't venture into the side bays or the cattail marsh at the lake's east end.

Other species found on Upper Beaver include Yellow-bellied and Olive-sided Flycatchers. Tree and Barn Swallows are always feeding over the water, along with some Chimney Swifts. Merlins nest along the south shore in the tall pines; listen for their whining when they have young. Geese have nested on the lake in recent years. Ducks that nest here are Wood Duck, Mallards, American Black Duck, and Common and Hooded Mergansers.

One of the best birding spots is the marsh and bog on the east side of the large island near the east end of the lake. It's home to Wilson's Snipe and American Bittern as well as ducks, geese, and loons. A large patch of buckbean blooms here in early June. Come July, the bog mat is covered with rose pogonias.

In the channels of the cattail marsh at the far eastern end of the lake, I've heard Sora and Virginia Rail but not seen them. This was where the first loon in New York received a satellite transmitter, in 2002. This bird, a male, left Beaver Lake that fall and wintered on the New Jersey coast. It returned the following summer (and in subsequent summers) and fathered a chick. We later recaptured the bird to remove the transmitter. **—GL**

52 Francis Lake

Watch the nesting Common Loons dive under a floating bog mat on this remote gem of a lake. Other species include Blue-headed Vireo, Mourning Warbler, Pine Warbler, Cedar Waxwing, Eastern Kingbird, Merlin, and Broad-winged Hawk.

DIRECTIONS: From NY 28 in Eagle Bay, drive north and west on Big Moose Road and Stillwater Road. After 18 miles, turn left at the stop sign near Stillwater, drive about 7 miles to a handicapped-access lot on the left, and park along the road. Much of the driving will be on dirt roads. You also can reach the put-in by driving east out of Lowville on Number Four Road. About 18 miles from Lowville, the road takes a sharp right and becomes Stillwater Road. Take the turn and go 0.9 miles to the put-in. See map, p. 178.

Francis Lake is a little jewel, but not many folks come here, perhaps because it's so far off the beaten path. I usually have the place to myself. There are two private camps, but the rest of the shoreline is public Forest Preserve. There are two primitive campsites on the shore.

Mourning Warblers have nested in the berry briars (on private land) across the road from the parking lot. I have heard them while unloading my canoe. I have found White-throated Sparrows and Blue-headed Vireos nesting along the short trail to the water.

The lake has a large floating bog mat that in late June is covered with thousands of blooming rose pogonias, pitcher plants, and sundews. Otters sometimes can be glimpsed playing in the bay behind the mat. White-throated, Song, and Swamp Sparrows nest on the mat and scold you as you

Photo by Phil Brown

Francis Lake

paddle by. Common Yellowthroat and Yellow-rumped Warbler nest in the mat's brushy areas.

In recent years, two Common Loons have nested near the mat, often swimming underneath to reach the main lake. Although they sometimes nested twice in a season, the loons successfully raised chicks only a few times in the five years I have watched them. Snapping turtles catch the chicks. Also, the otters may have stolen eggs (I once caught them right in the nest). These loons nest early, as they must prepare the chicks to migrate before the shallow lake freezes.

As you paddle around the lake, you'll hear many warblers singing. Pine and Nashville Warblers nest in or near the large white pines along the shore but are hard to spot. The Pine Warblers are the biggest singers. When there

Photo by Jeff Nadler

Eastern Kingbird

is a fly hatch, they join the Tree Swallows and Cedar Waxwings in catching bugs. Incidentally, you won't find blackflies on this lake, which distinguishes it from neighboring lakes. I suspect that the abundance of dragonflies and damselflies hatching on the bog mat has something to do with this. At times I've seen thousands of these predators in the air. In turn, several flycatchers feast on the dragonflies and damselflies. You can find Eastern Phoebes, Eastern Wood-Pewees, and Least Flycatchers near the camps and Olive-sided and Yellow-bellied Flycatchers on the far side of the mat.

A pair of Broad-winged Hawks has nested along the shoreline in recent years and often can be seen flying across the lake with food. Likewise, a pair of Merlins has been nesting either here or at nearby **Beaver Lake**. Eastern Kingbirds also nest along the lake sometimes, and if you get too close, they'll make a racket.

Francis Lake contains smallmouth bass, chain pickerel, and many species of small fish, so Common Mergansers often feed here. Mallards have nested near the outlet on the north end of the lake. **—GL**

⑤③ Tug Hill Wildlife Management Area

Bird right along the roads in search of Mourning Warbler, Scarlet Tanager, Rose-breasted Grosbeak, Winter Wren, hawks, ducks, all of the region's vireos, and lots of our warblers. Many boreal species reside here.

DIRECTIONS: From Lowville, go west (north) on NY 12 to NY 177. Bear left onto 177, which passes through a huge wind farm. Just past the wind turbines, take a left onto Sears Pond Road (there are some good birds here) and follow it to the Montague Inn. Go straight here on Parker Road. At the next intersection, you enter the Wildlife Management Area on Running George Road.

The Tug Hill Wildlife Management Area, located west of the Adirondack Park, is managed for timber and wildlife. The annual cutting produces good habitat for birds. Birds also frequent the beaver ponds found on the many streams. Many of the ponds lie within sight of the Wildlife Management Area's roads.

Gerry Smith, who surveyed this area in the 1980s for *The Atlas of Breeding Birds in New York State* and from 2000 to 2005 for its successor, told me that most of the species birders want to see can be found here. About the only ones you can't find are Gray Jay, Spruce Grouse, Bicknell's Thrush, and Blackpoll Warbler. Back in the 1980s, a Bay-breasted Warbler (a rare breeder in the Adirondacks) nested here. This certainly surprised me, but after birding this area several times, I realize that anything's possible.

Courtesy of New York State DEC

A wetland in the Tug Hill Wildlife Management Area

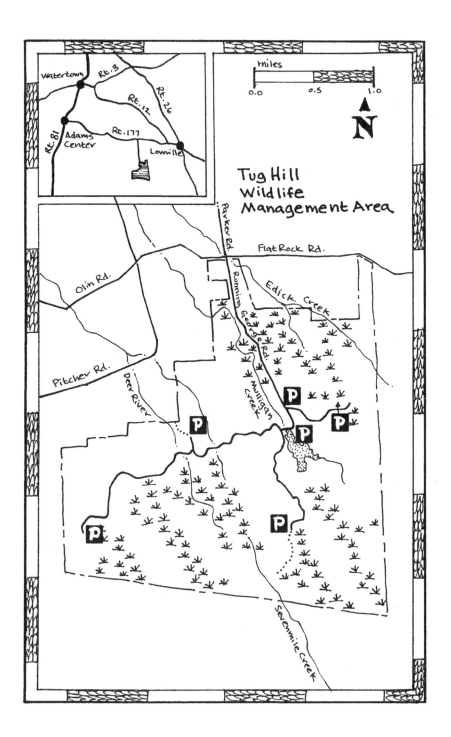

Most of the birding is done right along the seven miles of roads. If you wander into the woods (of which there are plenty), be sure to bring a map and compass. There aren't many landmarks in these rolling hills. I once flew over the region with Norton "Buster" Bird, an Adirondack bush pilot, and he told me that he would follow power lines or highways to find his way back to the Adirondacks in bad weather as there were no peaks to guide him.

I've visited the Wildlife Management Area a few times looking for rare orchids. On the fringes of the area, we found many showy lady's slippers and a broad-lipped twayblade, a flower that hadn't been seen in the state since 1923. While looking for orchids, I kept hearing Adirondack birds, including some hard-to-find ones. In the Adirondacks, you sometimes need to go a ways to find a Mourning Warbler, but the species occurs in abundance here. What great singers they are. You'll usually find them in the briars. You can find the other wood warblers here as well, along with the thrushes, Scarlet Tanager, Rose-breasted Grosbeak, Winter Wren, and several vireos, Red-eyed, Blue-headed, Philadelphia, and Yellow-throated. I don't see the Yellow-throated much up in the Adirondacks, but Gerry said it can be found near most of the water-bodies here.

When I visited in July 2007, I encountered seven families of Ruffed Grouse, one family of Wild Turkey, Northern Waterthrush feeding young, Olive-sided, Yellow-bellied, and Great Crested Flycatchers carrying food, most of the wood warblers, and Red-tailed and Broad-winged Hawks. Also, Pileated, Downy, and Hairy Woodpeckers, Northern Flicker, and Yellow-bellied Sapsucker (the last were most abun-

Photo by Jeff Nadler

Belted Kingfisher

dant). On the water I had Wood Duck, Ring-necked Duck, Mallard, Hooded Merganser, and Canada Goose. Belted Kingfishers were rattling near some of the ponds. In all, I counted nearly fifty species in three hours–including one that I didn't identify, so I have to go back. —**GL**

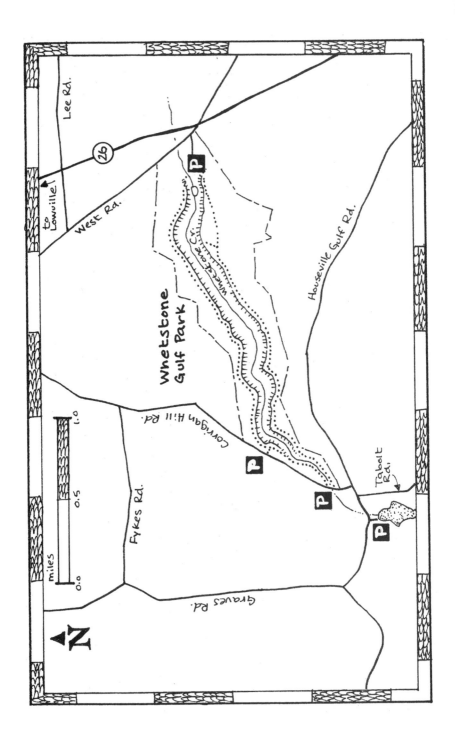

Whetstone Gulf

Soak up the scenery at this spectacular gorge before walking through the woods to find Hermit Thrush, Scarlet Tanager, Winter Wren, Rose-breasted Grosbeak, and warblers. Also check nearby fields for hawks and grassland species.

DIRECTIONS: From Lowville, drive south on NY 26 about 6 miles to West Road and turn right. The entrance to Whetstone Gulf State Park is just after the turn. If you're coming from the south, the turn off NY 26 is about 4 miles north of Turin. If you don't want to pay the entrance fee, continue north on West Road and turn left on Corrigan Hill Road. This road parallels the park boundary as it rises through farm fields. At 3 miles on the left is a plantation of Norway spruce. A marked trail leads a tenth of a mile from the road to the edge of the gulf. Farther up the road, there is a parking lot with access to the rim trail. If you continue on this road, you come to a T intersection. Take a right and go across Whetstone Gulf Stream; the next left takes you to Whetstone Gulf Reservoir.

Whetstone Gulf is a three-mile gorge that cuts through the eastern edge of the Tug Hill Plateau. It's described in the state park's brochure as the most spectacular scenic vista east of the Rocky Mountains; it's certainly worth a look-see. The park encompasses 2,100 acres, mostly wild. There are sixty-two campsites, a picnic area, and several trails. One of the trails circles the gorge; another goes right up the stream in the gorge. In winter, the roads and trails are used for cross-country skiing.

In the park proper are what I call yard birds: American Robin, Black-capped Chickadee, Chipping Sparrow, Eastern Phoebe, Wood Thrush, and Dark-eyed Junco. Once you leave the park landscape, you start hearing

Whetstone Gulf in winter

wood warblers, Hermit Thrush, Scarlet Tanager, Winter Wren, and Rose-breasted Grosbeak. The soil is limy, so the plant growth is lush. Jack-in-the-pulpits and red trilliums are three feet tall. Many kinds of ferns exist here, including Christmas and maidenhair. In one place periwinkle covers more than two acres of the forest floor.

Whetstone Gulf Reservoir is one of the few large bodies of water in this neck of the woods, so you'll find all kinds of waterbirds, such as American Black Duck, Mallard, Common and Hooded Mergansers, and Great Blue Heron. You can see only a small part of the reservoir from the shore, so it's advisable to bring a canoe or kayak. In dry falls, when the water level is low, you can expect to find sandpipers and other migrating shorebirds.

I found the best birding right along Corrigan Hill Road (which is unplowed in winter and used as a snowmobile trail). In the farm fields there are lots of Bobolink, Eastern Meadowlark, and Savannah Sparrow. Red-tailed Hawk, Northern Harrier, and American Kestrel hunt over the open fields. In the hedgerows are Yellow and Chestnut-sided Warblers, Gray Catbirds, and Common Yellowthroats. With all the planted evergreens this would also be a good place to catch some winter finches in a good cone year. Near the top of the road, I heard warblers, thrushes, and Winter Wren singing in the wooded areas. Not many birders have discovered this place, but it's enjoyable. **—GL**

Whetstone Creek at the state park's entrance

Southern Region

A Hodgepodge of Habitats

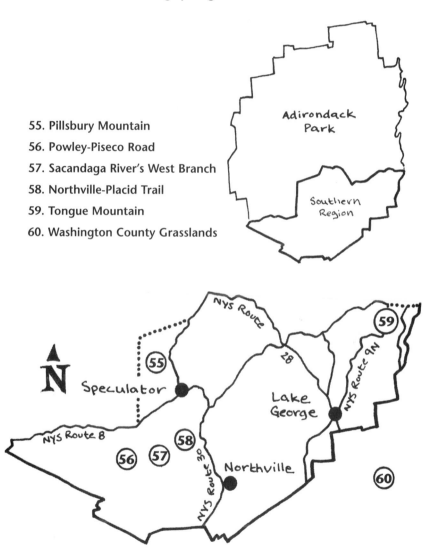

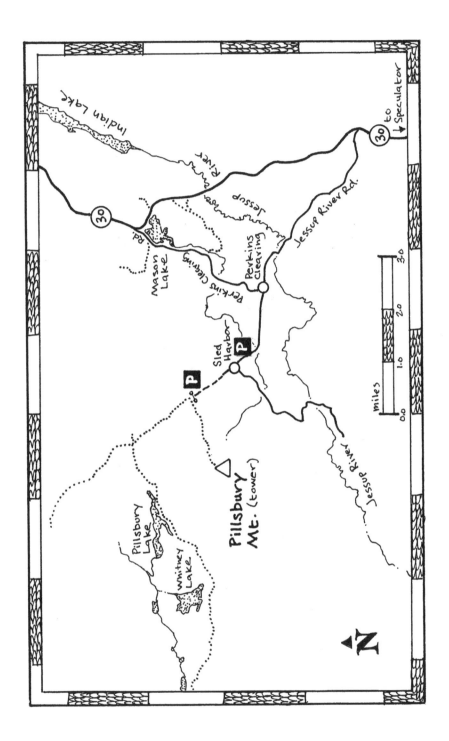

Pillsbury Mountain

Ascend one of the highest mountains in the central Adirondacks for a chance to find Bicknell's Thrush, Boreal Chickadee, Scarlet Tanager, Rose-breasted Grosbeak, and Blackpoll Warbler, among other birds. Great views from the fire tower.

DIRECTIONS: From the four corners in Speculator (the junction of NY 8 and NY 30), drive north on NY 30 for 8.3 miles to Perkins Clearing Road, a sharp left just past a roadside pull-off at Mason Lake. Follow this dirt road 3.3 miles to the junction marked by a DEC sign. Turn right and go 1.8 miles to another junction, just past the clearing at Sled Harbor. Turn right again and go 1.2 miles to the trailhead (the road now is narrower and rougher, so some people park at Sled Harbor). If driving south from Indian Lake, the turn for Perkins Clearing Road will be on the right, a few miles beyond Lewey Lake State Campground. Perkins Clearing Road is closed from December 1 to May 31. Don't try to drive to the trailhead via Jessup River Road as the bridge over the river is suitable only for snowmobiles.

Pillsbury Mountain is a good mountain to climb for the birds and the views. The birding begins well before you get to the trailhead. As you pass Mason Lake on Perkins Clearing Road, stop to look for a pair of nesting Common Loons. You'll also find interesting birds in the logged-over woods along the dirt road. In the many blackberry thickets, listen for the rich *churry, churry, churry, churry, chorry, chorry* of the Mourning Warbler. If you think you hear Red-eyed Vireos in the new aspens, be sure to check them out, because they may be Philadelphia Vireos (they sound the same to me).

Wetland along Perkins Clearing Road

Photo by Phil Brown

View from the Pillsbury Mountain tower

Chestnut-sided Warblers also love this habitat.

From the trailhead, it's a 1.6-mile hike to the fire tower on the summit, with a vertical ascent of 1,337 feet. You should find most of the Adirondack wood warblers along the trail as well as several thrushes (principally, the Hermit Thrush). Once you get in the bigger timber, you should hear Scarlet Tanager and Rose-breasted Grosbeak. Higher up, the songs of the wood warblers and Hermit Thrush give way to the high, thin *zi-zi-zi-zi-zi-zi-zi-zi-zi* of the Blackpoll Warbler and the *ch-ch zreee p-zreeew p-p-zreee* of the Bicknell's Thrush, a species much desired by birders. This reclusive bird breeds at high elevations in the Adirondacks and Catskills. At least three pairs of Bicknell's have been heard singing near the Pillsbury tower. Boreal Chickadee and Northern Saw-whet Owl also have been recorded in the thick evergreens on the mountaintop.

If you camp out on the summit, you'll hear the Bicknell's singing much of the night. Thrushes in the moonlight—what a beautiful sound! You can watch the sunset and sunrise from the tower's stairs. The tower also has the best view over the West Canada Wilderness, looking west to West, South and Mud lakes, north to the Cedar Lakes, and northeast to the Cedar River Flow.

Back at the trailhead, if you have the time, you might want to take the trail to Pillsbury and Whitney lakes, both good birding spots. It's 3.3 miles to the lean-to at Pillsbury Lake and almost two miles more to Whitney Lake. We once heard Cape May Warblers singing near Pillsbury Lake. That same day, Mike Peterson and I took a boat ride on Whitney, propelled by a couple of frying pans. We went to a solitary little island in the middle of the lake and saw a loon nest with two eggs, and not two feet away was a Mallard sitting on a nest with eggs. **—GL**

Powley-Piseco Road

Enjoy a pleasant drive on a dirt road through the forest, stopping to observe birds at wetlands, ponds, and streams. Among the species you may encounter are Olive-sided and Yellow-bellied Flycatchers, Lincoln's Sparrow, and American Three-toed Woodpecker.

DIRECTIONS: From the intersection of NY 8 and NY 10 near Piseco, drive south on NY 10 about a mile. Just after crossing Big Bay and Piseco Outlet, turn right onto Powley Road. You also can access the road's south end from NY 29A in Stratford, where it's known as the Piseco Road.

The Powley-Piseco Road stretches nineteen miles between Route 29A and Route 10. The northern section, which is dirt, offers the best birding. Most of the land along this part is in the public Forest Preserve. You can stop anywhere, as there is hardly any traffic. In season, I don't think you could get out of the car without hearing a few birds singing. The habitat varies from hardwoods to boggy areas to softwoods to old beaver ponds. There are several informal campsites along the way. The road is unplowed in winter, when it's used as a snowmobile route. It's usually passable by cars from mid-May until early December.

Starting from the north end, you'll reach a small pull-off on the left after about two miles. This is the start of a quarter-mile trail to Sand Lake. Although acid rain has killed the fish, the lake still has a pair of nesting loons, which raise their young on aquatic bugs, newts, and tadpoles. The trail often is a little wet in places but well worth the walk. Try a few Barred Owl calls, and you may get some answers.

At 3.7 miles from Route 10, you come to a small waterbody on the left, one of the many Mud Ponds in the Adirondacks. There is a campsite at the start of the unmarked trail. It's a short way down to the pond's quaking bog, where you'll find sphagnum moss, leatherleaf, cranberry, bog laurel, and other plants that thrive in an acidic environment. You may also find a few good birds, such as Olive-sided and Yellow-bellied Flycatchers and Lincoln's and White-throated Sparrows. Visitors should avoid trampling the bog mat.

At 8.2 miles, you reach a big open area known as Powley Place. There is a large marshy area on both sides of the road, a must for birders. American Three-toed Woodpecker nested here in 2000. In 2006, I received several reports of Olive-sided Flycatcher singing here (as well as other spots along the road). You can launch a canoe on the East Canada at the iron bridge and paddle in either direction, though you'll soon encounter lots of alders if you head upstream.

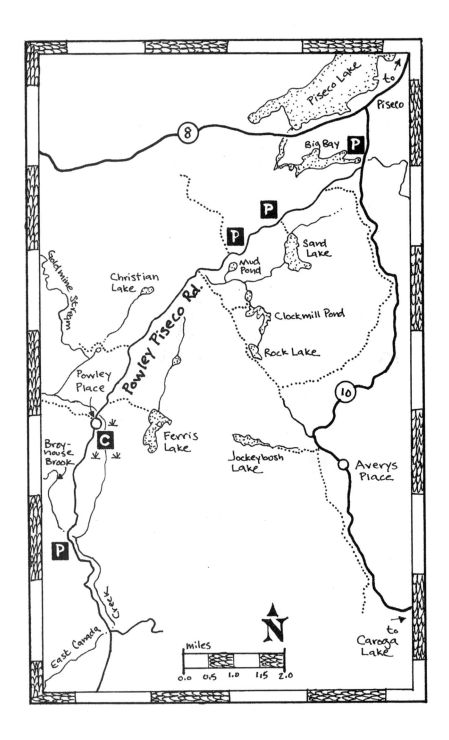

East Canada Creek

Eleven miles from Route 10, just before passing from Hamilton County to Fulton County, you'll come to Brayhouse Brook, another good place to check for birds, including Alder Flycatcher, Eastern Kingbird, and wood warblers. If you do stop, take a walk to the Potholers, where Brayhouse Brook meets the East Canada. The bubbling waters and pebbles have worn depressions in the rock streambed. The short path begins on the east side of the road.

If you have a canoe, you also might want to paddle Big Bay, an impoundment on Piseco Outlet, either before or after your drive on Powley-Piseco Road. You can put in at the Route 10 bridge. Big Bay has a pair of Common Loons, and Great Blue Herons usually can be seen feeding along the shore. Belted Kingfishers, warblers, and thrushes also can be heard or spotted along the water. It's possible to paddle from Big Bay into Piseco Lake. **—GL**

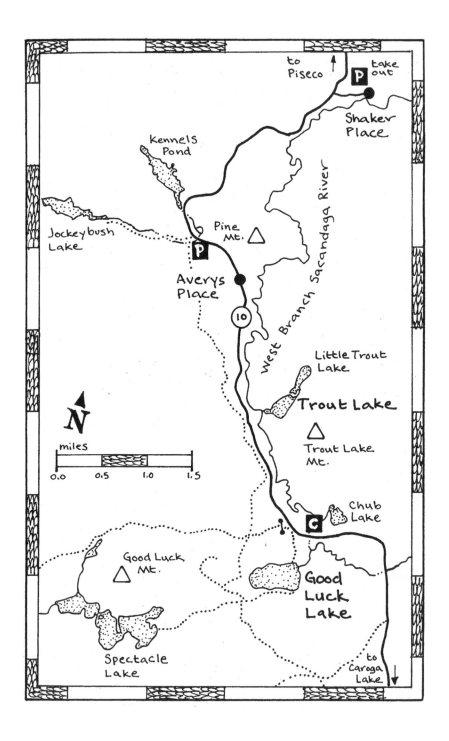

to Piseco

take out

P

Shaker Place

Kennels Pond

West Branch Sacandaga River

Pine Mt.

P

Averys Place

10

Jockeybush Lake

Little Trout Lake

Trout Lake

Trout Lake Mt.

N

miles
0.0   0.5   1.0   1.5

Chub Lake

G

Good Luck Mt.

Good Luck Lake

Spectacle Lake

to Caroga Lake

Sacandaga River's West Branch

Canoe on a tranquil river that meanders through marsh, alder swamp, and woods—habitat for a rich diversity of birds. Ducks, hawks, warblers, and most of the region's flycatchers and vireos dwell here. Bald Eagle also may be seen.

DIRECTIONS: From Caroga Lake, take NY 29A north to Pine Lake, where 29A turns west. Continue north on NY 10, crossing the West Branch of the Sacandaga River twice. Just after the second bridge, reached in six miles, pull into a parking area on the right. This is a put-in for canoeists. For the take-out, drive 6.5 miles farther north and turn right onto a dirt lane.

From the put-in on the West Branch of the Sacandaga River, you can paddle downriver about ten miles to Shaker Place, with optional side trips to Chub Lake and Trout Lake. It's all flatwater. If you go the entire distance, you'll want to spot a second car at the take-out. If you have only one car, just go part way and turn around. You're still bound to have a good day of birding.

The habitat varies from alders to open swamp to woods. You should find most of the flycatchers, Swamp and White-throated Sparrows, Yellow and Chestnut-sided Warblers, Common Yellowthroat, White-breasted Nuthatch, and Winter Wren. Be sure to check out all the vireo calls, as five species occur here: Blue-headed, Red-eyed, White-eyed, Philadelphia, and Yellow-throated (the last three less frequently). You also can expect to see Red-winged Blackbirds, Common Grackles, and Pileated, Hairy, and Downy Woodpeckers as well as most of the region's ducks. Watch and listen for Belted Kingfisher (one may even fish in front of your canoe). Broad-winged and Red-tailed Hawks, as well as Northern Harriers, often hunt the open areas. And Bald Eagle and Osprey are always a possibility when you're on an Adirondack waterway.

To get to Chub Lake, look for a tiny outlet on the right about a quarter-mile downriver from the bridge. You'll probably have to carry over a few beaver dams to reach the small lake. Wild cranberry and other bog plants grow along the shores. The short outlet to Trout Lake is reached about two miles from the put-in. Look for it on the right just north of Trout Lake Mountain. From Trout Lake, you can paddle into Little Trout Lake as well. In *Adirondack Canoe Waters: South and West Flow*, Alec Proskine writes that some paddlers saw a Golden Eagle at Trout Lake in September 1983. From the put-in, it's also possible to paddle upriver into Good Luck Lake.

If you're not paddling, you can still get in some good birding. The highway north of the put-in has a number of trailhead parking lots and other pull-offs that are close to the river, ponds, and beaver flows—all good

Negotiating a curve on the West Branch

bets for some birds. Near the ponds, you might see Northern Waterthrush, Spotted Sandpiper, and other species drawn to water. The hardwoods harbor most of the wood warblers and thrushes, and in some of the briars growing in cut-over areas you can hear the song of the Mourning Warbler: *churry, churry, churry, churry, chorry, chorry.*

While you're in the area, you might want to visit the Piseco Airport, where Eastern Bluebird and Savannah Sparrow occur along the runway. To get there, follow State Route 10 to State Route 8, turn right, and after 3.3 miles, turn left onto County Route 24. The airport will be on the right a few miles up the road. Also, look for a bog swamp on the south side of Route 8 before the Piseco turn. Many times Olive-sided Flycatcher and Wood Duck can be seen from the highway. **—GL**

Northville-Placid Trail

Hike a piece of the storied Northville-Placid Trail and search for birds that like the deep woods, such as Scarlet Tanager, Rose-breasted Grosbeak, and Barred Owl. You may find Olive-sided Flycatcher or Great Crested Flycatcher near wetlands.

DIRECTIONS: From NY 30 on the south side of the hamlet of Wells, turn west onto Algonquin Drive. Go 0.8 miles to West River Road on the left. This road goes 8.3 miles to the parking area near Whitehouse, the site of an old hotel. The Northville-Placid Trail passes through Whitehouse. The road, unplowed in winter, is usually open by mid-May.

The West River Road, which turns to dirt after a few miles, follows the West Branch of the Sacandaga River much of the way to Whitehouse. There is good birding along the road. Since this is the southern part of the Adirondack Park, you'll see many oaks, elms, and ash trees. Also, the Civilian Conservation Corps planted red pine, white pine, and Norway spruce along the road in the 1930s. The mix of trees creates habitat for a good variety of birds. In the poplars, look for Philadelphia Vireo (their song is much like that of the Red-eyed Vireo, but slower and sweeter). There are a few cleared lots that provide nesting places for many different warblers. Some clearings have camps where Eastern Phoebe, Eastern Wood-Pewee, and other flycatchers have been known to nest. Watch for Spotted Sandpiper among the rocks in the river.

The road climbs more than four hundred feet before descending slightly to Whitehouse. From the parking area, follow a well-trod path for a few minutes

A scene along West River Road

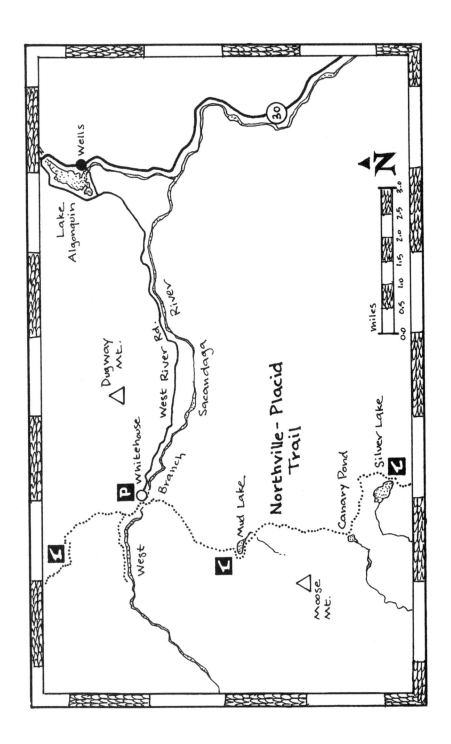

to the Northville-Placid Trail and a register. From here, you can hike south three miles to the Mud Lake lean-to, almost seven miles to Canary Pond (don't expect to see any canaries), or nine miles to the Silver Lake lean-to. If you camp out at one of these ponds, you can get up with birds.

Most of the time you'll have the trail to yourself. Soon after leaving the register, you'll cross the West Branch on a suspension bridge. The trail goes through a variety of forest habitat. You should find most of the wood warblers, thrushes, and flycatchers. Even this far south, if you come upon an old beaver pond with standing timber, you may hear the Olive-sided Flycatcher's *pip, pip, pip* in the morning or *quick-three-beers* in the afternoon or the *queep*! or *krreep* of the Great Crested Flycatcher. Pileated and Hairy Woodpeckers love these woods, as do Yellow-bellied Sapsuckers. If you find the circular line of holes of the sapsucker in a yellow birch, wait around awhile; even in deep woods, a Ruby-throated Hummingbird should show up to feed on insects attracted to sap in the holes.

Other birds that like big woods are Scarlet Tanager, Rose-breasted Grosbeak, and Barred Owl. On this trail, I'm owl calling all of the time, which attracts many birds. Occasionally, an owl will answer. If an owl comes in to investigate, remain very still, because it can detect the slightest movements. Owls hunt during the day when they have young to feed. In softwoods, use a Northern Saw-whet Owl call first–a series of toots, like the alarm on a truck backing up. Then try a Barred Owl call. If you do the Barred Owl call first, you'll never hear the saw-whet, because they don't like being eaten. **—GL**

The suspension bridge on the Northville-Placid Trail

Photo by Phil Brown

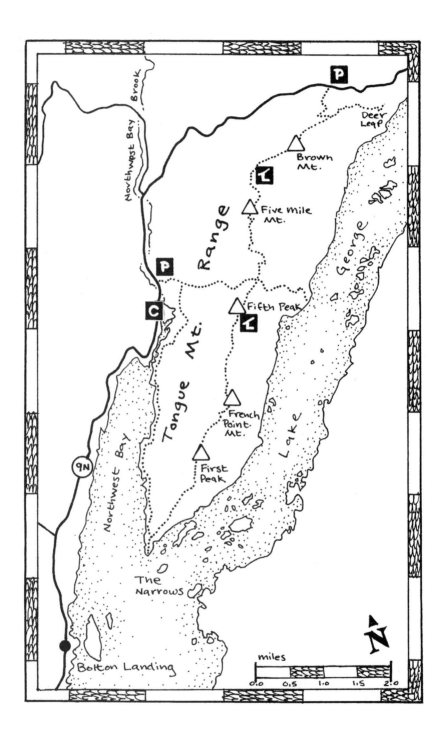

Map labels: Northwest Bay Brook, P, Deer Leap, Brown Mt., Five mile Mt., Range, P, C, Fifth Peak, George, Tongue Mt., French Point Mt., Lake, 9N, First Peak, Northwest Bay, The Narrows, Bolton Landing, N, miles, 0.0, 0.5, 1.0, 1.5, 2.0

59 Tongue Mountain & Northwest Bay Brook

Climb the Tongue for the stunning views of Lake George as well as for the birds. Thirteen species of warblers have been observed on the ridge. For waterbirds, take a short canoe trip through the marsh on Northwest Bay Brook.

DIRECTIONS: From Northway Exit 24, drive east on County 11 to NY 9N. Turn left and drive about four miles to a small parking area on the right. This is the canoe put-in for Northwest Bay Brook. Just up the road is a larger parking area at Clay Meadow for those hiking up Tongue Mountain or along the Northwest Bay Trail. There is another trailhead about six miles farther up the highway, on the left side. The trail there begins across the road.

Tongue Mountain is a long peninsula, with several peaks, that sticks out into Lake George. Most of the mountain is covered with hardwoods, including oaks, but some of the ridges have stands of big pines, both red and white. A word of caution about timber rattlesnakes: though rarely seen, they do live here. The snakes are timid, but you should be careful about where you step or put your hands. The only one I ever saw was when I was a kid, and that's going back a few years. Our family was driving to Roger's Rock State Campground on Lake George's northwest shore when we saw a rattler in the road.

The state maintains about twenty miles of trails on Tongue Mountain, some more rugged than others. For an easy outing, hike to Deer Leap, which is 1.7 miles from the northern trailhead. The trail passes through good bird habitat, including several beaver ponds (some old, some still active). Wood Ducks and Mallards breed at the ponds. Look also for wood warblers, vireos, thrushes, flycatchers, and woodpeckers.

From the northern trailhead, it's 11.4 miles to Montcalm Point, the tip of the Tongue. The ridgeline trail goes over a number of summits and passes two lean-tos, on Five Mile Mountain and Fifth Peak. It has many lookouts with views of Lake George. Peregrine Falcon, Merlin, Red-tailed Hawk, Osprey, and Turkey Vulture might be seen from any of these lookouts.

From the Clay Meadow parking lot, it's 5.4 miles to Montcalm Point, following the trail along the eastern shore of Northwest Bay. It's less than two miles to the marsh, which is filled with interesting birds (see below). You also can do a 13.4-mile loop from Clay Meadow, climbing up Fifth Peak, continuing over French Point Mountain and First Peak to the point, and then returning on the Northwest Bay Trail.

Photo by Carl Heilman II

Lake George spread out below Tongue Mountain

Whichever route you take, you're sure to pass through mature woods with lots of birds, including Pileated and Hairy Woodpeckers, Northern Flicker, Yellow-bellied Sapsucker, Scarlet Tanager, Rose-breasted Grosbeak, and Eastern Wood-Pewee. All told, thirteen warblers have been identified on Tongue Mountain, some in the woods, others in the wetlands at the base of the peak. Red Crossbills also nest in years with a bumper crop of cones in the red pines.

If you like to paddle, the mile-long trip down Northwest Bay Brook is a delight. You'll pass overhanging arrowwood and wild raisin, both berry-producing shrubs, in the first quarter-mile and wind through a marshland the rest of the way to the lake. Along the brushy banks before the marsh are Gray Catbird, Baltimore Oriole, American Redstart, Common Yellowthroat, Yellow and Chestnut-sided Warblers, and Warbling, Red-eyed and Blue-headed Vireos. In the marsh, look for Great Blue Heron, Least Bittern, Pied-billed Grebe, Wood Duck, Mallard, Hooded and Common Mergansers, Merlins nesting in the nearby pines, and White-throated, Song, and Swamp Sparrows.

Whether you take a hike on the hardwood ridge or paddle through the marsh, you're bound to see a satisfying variety of birds. And, if you're lucky, you might also get to see a rattlesnake. **—GL**

⑥⓪ Washington County Grasslands

Take a drive on country roads to find grassland species now at risk in New York, such as Upland Sandpiper, Sedge Wren, and Vesper Sparrow. The visitors in winter include Short-eared Owl and Rough-Legged Hawk.

DIRECTIONS: The heart of the grasslands can be reached from the village of Fort Edward by driving south on US 4 or east on NY 197 and from the village of Hudson Falls by driving east on NY 196. See the accompanying map for local roads within the region.

Years ago, natural grasslands existed in only a few places in New York State, such as Long Island, the lower Hudson Valley, and the Finger Lakes region. The clearing of lands for agriculture greatly expanded the habitat for grassland birds. But as New York farmers have gone out of business, selling their fields for development or simply allowing them to grow back into woods, the populations of many grassland species have dropped sharply. State wildlife officials estimate that the abundance of certain birds, such as Henslow's Sparrow and Northern Harrier, has declined more than eighty percent since the 1960s.

Fortunately, the state Department of Environmental Conservation is taking steps to preserve one of the most significant grassland habitats in northern New York. The Washington County Grasslands encompass thirteen thousand acres of croplands, pastures, wetlands, and small woodlots east of the villages of Fort Edward and Hudson Falls, just south of the Adirondack Park. In 2007, DEC announced plans to preserve four thousand acres in the core of this region, through the purchase of land and the acquisition of conservation easements. DEC hopes to control development, manage the lands to protect grassland birds, and provide recreational access. The agency is planning to build a bird-observation platform and blind.

The Washington County Grasslands harbor several breeding species at risk in New York, including Northern Harrier, Upland Sandpiper, Sedge Wren, and Vesper,

Photo by Jeff Nadler

Grasshopper Sparrow

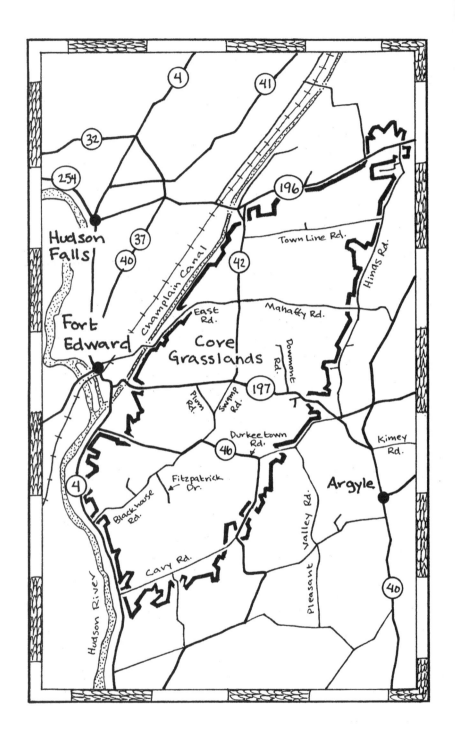

Grasslands east of Fort Edward

Grasshopper and Henslow's Sparrows (the last is uncommon). Other summer birds include American Kestrel, Red-tailed Hawk, Killdeer, Bobolink, Savannah Sparrow, Eastern Meadowlark, and Orchard Oriole.

The region also is important for winter raptors, most notably Short-eared Owl, which is listed as endangered in New York, and Rough-legged Hawk. Peregrine Falcons have been seen hunting from silos and devouring prey on utility poles. Among the other species that may turn up in winter are Horned Lark, Northern Shrike, Snow Bunting, Common Redpoll, and Lapland Longspur. In January and February 2008, birders kept tabs on an immature Snowy Owl. That same winter, a Merlin was spotted on top of a telephone pole on January 26. A flock of three thousand migrating Snow Geese was seen near Durkeetown Road on March 27, 2002.

Since most of the grasslands remains in private hands, birding is usually done along the country roads. Mona Bearor, who edits the newsletter for the Southern Adirondack Audubon Society, recommends the following roads, both for grassland species and for winter raptors: Cary, Blackhouse, Fitzpatrick, Swamp, Mahaffy, and Hinds. Those looking for Short-eared Owls should focus on Blackhouse, Fitzpatrick, and Plum roads.

The National Audubon Society has designated the region an Important Bird Area (which it calls the Fort Edward Grasslands). In recent years, the region has come under increasing pressure for development. Let's hope that the state and local governments, working with environmental groups, will be able to buck the trend so the grasslands will continue to deserve the designation for generations to come. —**Phil Brown**

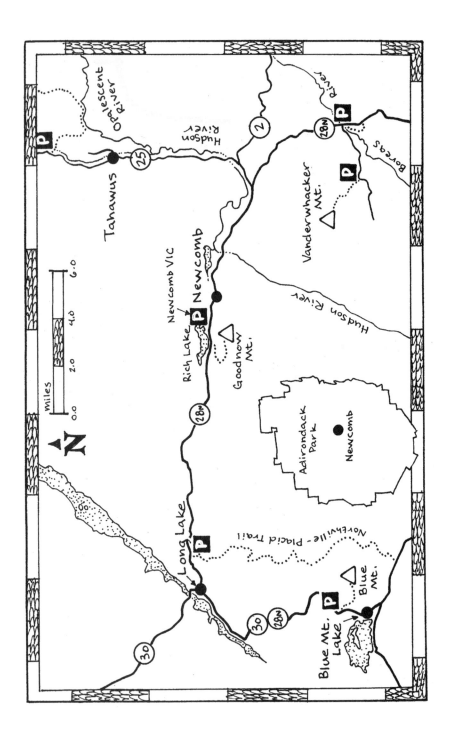

Bonus Sites: Route 28N Corridor

The 25-mile highway corridor from Minerva to Newcomb to Long Lake contains an abundance of boreal habitat where birders can find desirable species. The following four sites could all be birded in a day, but if time is limited try the Newcomb VIC.

Boreas River. A pleasant walk along the Boreas through habitat where you can find northern birds, including Blacked-backed Woodpecker and Boreal Chickadee, as well as lots of warblers. At the Route 28N bridge where the hike begins, look for species of more open habitat and for Eastern Phoebe or Barn Swallow under the bridge. Hike 1.2 miles to Hewitt Eddy and turn around, or else walk another 0.8 miles to another spot on the highway and then return. DIRECTIONS: The NY 28N bridge is 8.7 miles north of Minerva.

Vanderwhacker Mountain. Expect to find Canada Warbler in the first mile or so of the 2.7-mile trail. A wetland created by beavers is reached at 0.7 miles and another at 0.9 miles. Olive-sided Flycatcher, Lincoln's Sparrow, and Rusty Blackbird have been seen at both. Beyond the wetlands, the trail starts to steepen. Those who make the 1,650-foot ascent to the summit may encounter Yellow-bellied Flycatcher and Boreal Chickadee. The fire tower offers a superb view of the High Peaks. DIRECTIONS: From Minerva, drive north on NY 28N; just after crossing the Boreas River, turn left onto a dirt road and go 2.6 miles to trailhead on right.

Newcomb VIC. The state Visitor Interpretive Center in Newcomb, open 9 a.m. to 5 p.m., has 3.6 miles of trails. Occasionally, Common Loon occurs on Rich Lake or Black-backed Woodpecker along the trails. The VIC also is a good place to search for winter finches such as Purple Finch, both crossbills, Common Redpoll, Pine Siskin, and Evening Grosbeak. After birding, warm up inside while enjoying the natural-history exhibits. DIRECTIONS: The VIC is about a mile west of Newcomb's hamlet and about 12 miles east of Long Lake.

Northville-Placid Trail (Long Lake). Explore boreal and deciduous habitat on an easy section of the NP and connecting ski trails. In the first half-mile, which is mostly boreal, look for Black-backed Woodpecker, Alder and Yellow-bellied Flycatchers, Gray Jay, Boreal Chickadee, and Ruby-crowned Kinglets. Warblers may include Nashville and Northern Parula from May to September. The next half-mile of mixed and deciduous woods may have Broad-winged Hawk, Swainson's and Hermit Thrushes, a variety of wood warblers (Chestnut-sided, Black-throated Blue, Black-throated Green, and Blackburnian), and Scarlet Tanager. DIRECTIONS: From the junction of NY 28N and NY 30 in Long Lake, drive 1.5 miles east on 28N to a parking area on the right. Take the trail south.

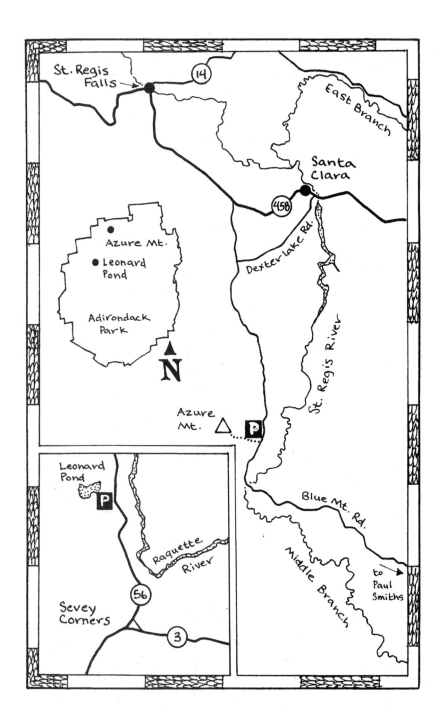

St. Regis Falls

14

East Branch

Santa Clara

458

Dexter Lake Rd.

Azure Mt.

Leonard Pond

Adirondack Park

N

St. Regis River

Azure Mt. △ P

Leonard Pond P

Raquette River

56

Sevey Corners

3

Blue Mt. Rd.

Middle Branch

to Paul Smiths

Bonus Sites: A Final Four

Blue Mountain. This popular peak has one of the largest populations of Bicknell's Thrush in the Adirondacks. The two-mile trail ascends 1,550 feet to a fire tower with superb views. Many warbler species can be found along the trail, including Canada in wet thickets at lower elevations and Blackpoll on the upper portion of the mountain. Other woodland birds often seen or heard are Eastern Wood-Pewee, Yellow-bellied Flycatcher, Blue-headed Vireo, Boreal Chickadee, Winter Wren, Golden-crowned Kinglet, and Swainson's Thrush. DIRECTIONS: From junction of NY 28 and NY 30 in Blue Mountain Lake, drive north on NY 30 for 1.4 miles to trailhead on right. See map, p. 208.

Tahawus. A fairly easy trail in the High Peaks Wilderness leads from the Hudson River to the Opalescent River, passing Lake Jimmy and Lake Sally. Much of the forest is recovering from storm damage—good habitat for birds. Among the species to be seen are Common Loon, Olive-sided Flycatcher, Boreal Chickadee, and many warblers, including Nashville, Magnolia, and Canada. The trail goes all the way to the Flowed Lands, but most birders turn around after reaching the Opalescent, if not before. DIRECTIONS: East of Newcomb, take Rt. 25 north and park in lot on the right just past old stone blast furnace. See map, p. 208.

Azure Mountain. Species observed from the summit of this small mountain in the northern Adirondacks include Turkey Vulture, Peregrine Falcon, and Common Raven. Golden Eagle and hawks are often seen during fall migration. At the trailhead, listen for Black-backed Woodpecker in the conifers. On the trail, look for Mourning Warbler and Indigo Bunting in berry thickets. Blackpoll Warbler dwells on the summit. The one-mile trail ascends to a refurbished fire tower. On the drive to the trailhead from the north, stop at wet woods bordering the road to look for Northern Waterthrush and Canada Warbler. If approaching from the south, see **Madawaska** for birding stops on the way. DIRECTIONS: From NY 458, 4 miles west of St. Regis Falls, drive south on Blue Mountain Road for about 7 miles to a parking area on the right. Or from Paul Smiths, turn off NY 30 onto Keese Mill Road and go 18.2 miles. Much of Blue Mountain Road is dirt.

Leonard Pond. Old dirt roads lead through boreal habitat and conifer stands. Look for Black-backed Woodpecker, Gray Jay, and Boreal Chickadee right from the start. Northern Saw-whet Owl, both crossbills, and Evening Grosbeak are some other species that can be found. The trail comes to a junction after 0.9 miles. Turn left, go another 1.3 miles to a gate, and turn around. Some of the best boreal habitat is toward the end. Near the junction, look for paths to the pond. DIRECTIONS: From NY 3 at Sevey Corners (east of Cranberry Lake), drive north on NY 56 for 2.5 miles and look for an unmarked dirt road on the left.

Finding Boreal Birds

Many birders have a special interest in boreal, or northern, species that in New York State nest primarily in the Adirondacks. Following is a list of our boreal breeders and their favorite habitats. Both authors are "habitat birders." We have found from experience—including a dozen years of field-work for breeding-bird atlases—that the best way to find a species is to search its habitat in many places rather than look for it at one or two locations. We have included a few suggested sites for each species, but think of these only as starting points. Knowledge of habitat is the real key to finding birds.

Spruce Grouse: Immature or uneven-aged spruce-fir stands; males display in larger conifers with open understory; hens nest in open areas with mosses, lichens, shrubs; roosts where trees are closely spaced; may move to upland spruce forests with blueberries in summer. **Massawepie Mire, Spring Pond Bog, Shallow Lake.**

American Three-toed Woodpecker: Dead timber after fires or logging; spruce bogs with standing dead trees; mountain spruce-fir; feeds mainly on bark beetles by flaking. **High Peaks, Shallow Lake, Osgood River.**

Gray Jay

Black-backed Woodpecker: Wet areas in both mountain spruce-fir and spruce-balsam-northern hardwoods with recently killed timber; feeds mainly on wood-boring beetles by drilling; nest holes of both boreal woodpeckers have beveled bottom lips. **California Road & Debar Pond, Paul Smiths VIC, Third Lake Creek.**

Olive-sided Flycatcher: Small boggy ponds, swampy ends of lakes, marshy streams, river backwaters, quaking bogs, old beaver meadows in coniferous or mixed forest with dead snags for perches. **Bloomingdale Bog, Chubb River Swamp, Powley-Piseco Road.**

Illustration by Mike Storey

Yellow-bellied Flycatcher: Young stands of spruce forest, dense and shady with ground cover of moss; low black spruce from 1,800 feet to high-elevation red spruce in High Peaks. **Francis Lake, Pillsbury Mountain, Raquette Lake Inlets.**

Philadelphia Vireo: Deciduous second-growth in the wake of fires or logging, dominated by quaking aspen, sometimes yellow birch or sugar maple; generally 1,500 to 2,600 feet in the Adirondacks. **Hurricane Mountain, Marcy Dam Trail, Northville-Placid Trail at Whitehouse.**

Gray Jay: Medium to mature spruce forest, especially black spruce; occurs in white and red spruces, but found most often in lower-elevation black; nests in thick stands of moderate-size trees. **Bigelow Road, Madawaska, Wheeler Pond Loop.**

Boreal Chickadee: Mixed spruce and balsam fir, sometimes mixed with yellow birch, the dead stubs often used for nest cavities. **Chubb River Swamp, Ferd's Bog, High Peaks.**

Ruby-crowned Kinglet: Medium to mature spruce (especially white), sometimes with balsam fir; boreal bog forest to mixed woodland with spruces. **Adirondak Loj Road, Five Ponds Wilderness, Silver Lake Bog.**

Bicknell's Thrush: Montane red spruce and balsam fir from as low as 2,750 feet (Lake Colden) through the tree line, where black spruce replaces red, up to krummholz and rock summits. **Lyon Mountain, High Peaks, Whiteface Highway.**

Tennessee Warbler: Wet deciduous second growth, often quaking aspen, mixed with fir, spruce, tamarack, northern shrubs, and ground cover of sphagnum mosses; usually near open edge. **Cedar River Flow, Raquette Lake Inlets, Spring Pond Bog.**

Cape May Warbler: Medium-aged spruce, from 25-75 years old, usually with some regeneration of balsam fir; favors areas infested with spruce budworm. **Pillsbury Mountain, Riverside Drive, Whitney Wilderness.**

(Yellow) Palm Warbler: Open boreal bogs carpeted with sphagnum mosses, dotted with stunted black spruces and heath shrubs. **Massawepie Mire, Paul Smiths VIC, Shallow Lake.**

Bay-breasted Warbler: Coniferous or mixed growth of balsam fir, hemlock, pine, birch, willows, and shrubs; rivers, sluggish streams, beaver ponds; favors spruce budworm infestations. **Chubb River Swamp, High Peaks, Moose River Plains.**

Blackpoll Warbler: Montane forests of red spruce upward into subalpine zone of stunted fir and black spruce, almost to summits on southeastern exposures; sometimes found as low as 1,720 feet (Boreas River) in conifer forest, or even in sugar maple hardwood (Sled Harbor). **High Peaks, Pillsbury Mountain, Whiteface Highway.**

Wilson's Warbler: Wet beaver meadows, old pastures, bog pockets with surrounding willow, alder, spruce, tamarack, and fir; clearings with open spaces between clumps of meadowsweet or spirea; ground cover of moss and lichen. **Bloomingdale Bog, Madawaska.**

Lincoln's Sparrow: Fairly open areas with low and scattered black spruce and tamarack; bogs and fens; old clearings, abandoned fields and rail grades, roadsides and streamsides. **Five Ponds Wilderness, South Inlet, Wheeler Pond Loop.**

Rusty Blackbird: Boreal bogs, marshes, ponds, streamsides, swamps, and beaver meadows and ponds, all surrounded by forest and often with dead or dying standing trunks. **Chubb River Swamp, Peavine Swamp, Powley-Piseco Road.**

White-winged Crossbill: Fairly mature conifer forest with favored food trees (white spruce, tamarack, white pine), often near openings (roads, bogs, river corridors, abandoned rail grade); winter roads with salt and sand; especially abundant in years of bumper cone crops. **Cedar River Flow, Bigelow Road, Riverside Drive.**

–J.M.C.P

How to distinguish a Raven from a Crow

RAVEN
(bigger than a crow)

CROW
1 • Bowler Hat
2 • Vest & Bow Tie
3 • Cigar
4 • Spats

J. RUSSELL

Illustration by Jerry Russell

Suggested Reading

The dozen works below, together with the current volume, constitute a solid reference library on regional birds. Most of the recent works are in print, and information on ordering can be found on the publishers' Web sites. The older works that are out of print can often be found on Amazon or eBay or in used-book outlets. Comments are offered to assist the reader in selecting those that might be most useful. –J.M.C.P.

Andrle, Robert F. and Janet R. Carroll, eds. *The Atlas of Breeding Birds in New York State*. Ithaca and London: Cornell University Press, 1988.

The basic book on distribution and history of nesting birds, based upon 1980-85 fieldwork; landscape format, with species accounts and maps on facing pages. Strong in historical coverage, especially valuable for discussion of boreal species. 242 species and three hybrids.

Beehler, Bruce McP. *Birdlife of the Adirondack Park*. Glens Falls: Adirondack Mountain Club, 1978.

Well-done coverage of birds within the Blue Line, but showing its age. Still superb introductory essays on Park history, ecology, population trends, and the future of Adirondack birdlife by a leading ornithologist, written early in his career. 261 species.

Brown, Phil et mult. al. *Wild Neighbors: A Window on Adirondack Wildlife*. Saranac Lake, NY: *Adirondack Explorer*, 2007.

Includes forty-four articles on birds and birding that appeared in Adirondack Explorer *between 1998-2007, written for a general audience but containing much timely information.*

Bull, John. *Birds of New York State*. Garden City: Doubleday/Natural History Press, 1974. (Reprinted by Cornell University Press, Ithaca, NY, 1985.)

Still the best of the four major works on all birds of the state. Original 1974 edition hardbound; 1985 reprint softbound. Many of the gaps in knowledge of Adirondack birds that Bull lamented have been filled, but his often-opinionated style remains a model of clarity. Excellent maps of known distribution and banding recoveries, and color plates by noted artists. 410 species.

Carleton, Geoffrey and John M.C. Peterson, ed. *Birds of Essex County, New York*, 3rd ed. Elizabethtown, NY: High Peaks Audubon Society, Inc., 1999.

The basic reference on birds of the county. Information on status, seasonality and extreme dates, and maxima, supported by initials of observers. Thumbnail descriptions of twenty-one birding areas, several cliff sites and hawk watches not covered by the current authors. 310 species.

Drennan, Susan Roney. *Where to Find Birds in New York State: The Top 500 Sites*. Syracuse, NY: Syracuse University Press, 1981.

A longtime reference on birding areas; text and maps somewhat dated in places, but still useful. Interesting Foreword by Roger Tory Peterson.

The Kingbird. New York State Ornithological Association (formerly Federation of New York State Bird Clubs, Inc.). Vols. 1-58 (1950-2008), et seq.

The long-respected ornithological journal of New York State, published quarterly. Includes articles, notes and comments, "Highlights of the Season," and seasonal reports from the ten state regions, including Adirondack-Champlain Region 7. NYSOA membership also brings the newsletter New York Birders; *see the NYSOA website: www.nybirds.org.*

Levine, Emanuel, ed. ***Bull's Birds of New York State.*** Ithaca and London: Cornell University Press, 1998.

The "New Bull," most recent of the four major works on state birds. Species accounts written by a variety of authors, and treatment is rather uneven, but still a standard reference. Foreword by birder George E. Pataki and good prefatory material on a variety of subjects. 451 species.

McGowan, Kevin J. and Kimberley Corwin, eds. ***The Second Atlas of Breeding Birds in New York State:*** Ithaca and London: Cornell University Press, 2008.

The latest book on distribution and population trends of nesting birds, based upon 2000-05 fieldwork; portrait format, with species accounts and comparative maps on facing pages. Strong on changes and trends in birdlife, but less history than in the first atlas. 251 species.

Mitchell, Charles W. and William E. Krueger. ***Birds of Clinton County***, 2nd ed.. Elizabethtown, NY: High Peaks Audubon Society, Inc., 1997.

The basic reference on birds of the county. Species accounts follow a prose format; year dates and observers frequently omitted. Good descriptions of eighteen birding areas shown on three maps. 284 species. A 2006 First Supplement lists 310 species.

Peterson, John M.C. ***Birds of Franklin County, New York*** (with accompanying Birding Trail Map). Malone, NY: County of Franklin, 2006.

The basic reference on birds of the county. Status, seasonality and extreme dates, and maxima follow the format established by Carleton in 1976. Appendix and Birding Trail Map include reprints of 1877 Roosevelt & Minot List; map describes a dozen birding areas. Free from Franklin County Tourism (800-709-4895) upon request. 280 species.

Peterson, John M.C. and Gary N. Lee. ***Birds of Hamilton County, New York*** (with accompanying Birding Trail Map). Lake Pleasant, NY: County of Hamilton, 2004.

The basic reference on birds of the county. Status, seasonality and extreme dates, and maxima follow the Carleton format. Accompanying Birding Trail Map describes a dozen birding areas. Free from Hamilton County Tourism (800-648-5239) upon request. 238 species.

Index of Birds

Species are listed alphabetically by their common names. Because it would have been impractical to list all the pages where each species is mentioned, the numbers refer to the site chapters in the Table of Contents. Occasionally, page numbers are also provided for references that occur outside the site chapters.

Photo by Phil Brown

John M.C. Peterson (known as Mike) has served as the Adirondack-Champlain editor of *The Kingbird*, the journal of the New York State Ornithological Association, since 1982. He wrote "The History of Ornithology and Birding in New York State" as well as twelve species accounts of boreal birds for *The Second Atlas of Breeding Birds in New York State* (2008). He also authored *Birds of Franklin County* (2006), co-authored, with Gary N. Lee, *Birds of Hamilton County* (2004), and edited the third edition of *Birds of Essex County* (1999), written by his mentor, Geoffrey Carleton. He also has written articles on birds for *Adirondack Explorer*, *Adirondack Life*, *The Conservationist*, *New York Birders*, and *The Kingbird*. Mike served as the wildlife manager of the Four Brothers, a bird sanctuary on Lake Champlain, from 1982 to 2003. He is a master bander who has banded more than 73,000 birds, representing 162 species. He is one of the most successful birders in the Adirondack-Champlain region, having seen 279 species. Mike holds a bachelor's degree in English from Hobart College. After service as an Air Force officer, he did graduate work at the universities of Vermont and Rochester. He was an English professor at the Rochester Institute of Technology. He lives with his wife, Susan, in Elizabethtown and Montreal. They have two children and a granddaughter.

Photo courtesy of Gary Lee

Gary N. Lee, one of the Adirondacks' most adventurous birders, served as a New York State forest ranger for 35 years, working in the Moose River Plains and West Canada Lakes Wilderness. Since his retirement in 1999, he has monitored and banded loons every year for the Adirondack Loon Cooperative Program. He was a volunteer birder for *The Atlas of Breeding Birds in New York State* (1988) and its successor, *The Second Atlas of Breeding Birds in New York State* (2008) He also has helped band birds at Crown Point and the Four Brothers Islands. He co-authored, with John M.C. Peterson, *Birds of Hamilton County* (2004). He has written a weekly newspaper column, often focusing on birds and other wildlife, since 1986, first for the *Adirondack Express*, later for *Adirondack Weekly*. For decades, Gary has been watching and photographing birds wherever he travels: Hawaii, Florida, Colorado, Wyoming, Arizona, among other places. His life list for the Adirondack-Champlain region stands at 250 species. His photographs of birds have been published in *Adirondack Life*. Gary is a graduate of the New York State Ranger School in Wanakena. In 2000, he started an eco-tourism business, Daybreak to Twilight Tours. He lives in Inlet with his wife, Karen. They have three children and four grandchildren.

Jeff Nadler is a freelance nature photographer with a special interest in birds of the Northern Forest. His images have appeared in *Bird Watchers Digest*, *The Conservationist*, *Adirondack Life*, and *Adirondack Explorer*, among other publications. He takes many photographs of birds at risk. His work has been used by conservation and educational organizations, such as Audubon New York, the U.S. Forest Service, the National Geographic Society, the Wildlife Conservation Society, and the Boreal Songbird Initiative. Jeff spends much of his free time in the Adirondacks. Besides taking photographs, he enjoys paddling, hiking, and camping. He and his wife, Christine, live in Burnt Hills, a little south of the Adirondack Park. Jeff's work can be found online at www.jnphoto.com.